MW01036751

A Prairie Farm Boy Looks Over his Shoulder

A Prairie Farm Boy Looks Over his Shoulder

Orville G. Hiepler PH.D

© 2015 Orville G. Hiepler PH.D
All rights reserved.

ISBN: 1507804326
ISBN 13: 9781507804322
Library of Congress Control Number: 2015901782
CreateSpace Independent Publishing Platform
North Charleston, South Carolina

Bible verses used throughout this book are taken from the New International Version

This book is dedicated to my daughter Dorene who motivated and inspired me to share these stories from my life and helped make this book a reality.

CONTENTS

FOREWORD

Through the years, I have heard story after story from my dad about his growing-up years, his friends, and his many life experiences. Not until just recently had I heard the even more in-depth, interesting insights and incidents from his life and what they meant to him. I expressed to him that he was a good writer and asked him to please record the events he had told me so that we could pass them on to our children and friends. With much urging, suggesting, and nudging, Dad, at ninety-four years of age, has collected and written stories I have found encouraging, heartwarming, tear producing, newsworthy, or sometimes just plain ordinary. These took place during the ninety-four years of his life and the sixty-nine years of marriage he and Mom have shared.

Our purpose in sharing these stories with you is for you to enjoy his zest for life, to be inspired, and to gain insight into his thoughts and beliefs. He has been a role model to many.

With ninety-four years of blessings and sixty-nine years of ministry and marriage, there are many, many dear friends and family who could have been included in the stories. Everyone is important to my dad, but not every person from every experience and congregation could be included. My dad, together with Ilene, Mark, and me, has selected and compiled many of the ordinary to extraordinary life experiences he has had. Mom and Dad have centered their lives on the Lord Jesus Christ, and His grace and love have filled them with continued blessings.

—Dorene McDougall, daughter of the author

ACKNOWLEDGMENTS

Many have helped and contributed to the writing of this book. I thank these people for their contributions and support: Pastor John Kent, Pastor Ollie Olson, Pastor Robert Bradberry, Mr. John Brewer, Captain David Zinger, Dr. Curt McDougall, Carrone Van Nyhus, Beverly Lusk, Carmen Lusk, Jane Skuba, Anne Sturgell, the family of Sina Berg, the family of Don English, the family of Robert Loranger, Dale Homuth, Walt Lusk, Shelene Bryan, Michelle Hiepler, Kari Bradberry, Ryan Hiepler, Mark Hiepler, Ilene Hiepler Bradberry, and Dorene Hiepler McDougall.

The proceeds from this book will go toward educational and camp scholarships.

INTRODUCTION

It is almost unbelievable that so much can happen in one lifetime. When I was in sixth grade, my sister drove me to school four and a half miles away—a forty-five-minute ride in a horse and buggy. Now, ninety years later, my General Motors vehicle can take me forty-five miles to the Burbank Airport in about forty-five minutes; there, I step into a sleek aircraft going six hundred miles an hour and arrive in Phoenix, Arizona, some hundreds of miles away for my speaking engagement about forty-five minutes later.

When I started school, our otherwise sufficient home had no electric lights, no running water, no radio, and not even a telephone. Within two decades, we had all of the above. Wow! Within another thirty years, we had all of the above plus computers, TV, and you name it. And I currently hold in my hand a little package called a phone, which is also a camera, TV, radio, and more.

By His grace, God provided for me, a schoolboy who would get sick in the stomach when speaking in front of ten students in a one-room school and forty-five years later would speak three times each Sunday to hundreds of people at worship services. Among the churches I have served as CEO or senior pastor, one had a congregation of over twenty-seven hundred with a staff of sixty, many being pastors and schoolteachers. I served as principal, counselor, custodian, preacher, organizer, shepherd, and student, utilizing creativity, many talented friends, and any other available assets to achieve our goals. After relating some of my experiences, some would say, "Oh, that's impossible," but it wasn't. I worked hard and knew *Es muss gehen*, which is German for "It must go." The word *impossible* is not used by God.

In this book I will go into more detail about what I consider to be the ordinary walk that God has proposed for me; however, others have called much of it an extraordinary and even unbelievable journey.

May these stories help you to see how, in a successful world, in a worthwhile life, in our wonderful America, we never have to lose or give up on our zest for life and our experience of new adventures.

The Lord has provided all the ingredients for us to live this life to the fullest as we serve Him and our fellow humans. We need to use the gifts He has given us. We can do that only as we help other people in their journeys to find their best, their success, and their eternal happiness. I'm not sure if there is any real happiness unless we help others in finding real life and adventure. Reasons to cry, to laugh, to be frightened, and to be comforted will be further revealed in this book.

I will share some frightening and shocking events that happened without any slips, errors, or wrongdoing on my part. Life is just that way! No one knows what the future holds for us but I find comfort from the following passage.

"The Lord is my refuge in time of trial; He cares for those who trust in Him" (Nahum 1:7).

CHAPTER 1

BEGINNINGS

HOW IT ALL STARTED—EXTRAORDINARY

It was June 1, 1910
A neighbor asked, "Who is that happy and playful young couple riding north past the Westfall's homestead on those spirited horses?" (This would attract the attention of any observer.) Their fun included loosening the reins and permitting their youthful horses to go from a casual trot into a fast gallop as the bride playfully taunted the groom that her horse was faster than his.

The bride had become the proud owner of her first horse. This was the first time in her life that she'd actually had a riding horse. This one would be her very own. It was among the wedding gifts received from the groom. It was equivalent in 1910 to a LeBaron Chrysler roadster (sunroof and all) in 1999.

They quickly reined in their horses as they saw a new gully—a big wash—in front of John Olson's homestead shack. The bride held back Queen, her gray mare, and turned her to go around the deep gulley. The cowboy homesteader had another idea. He kicked his spurs into the side of his gallant bay gelding, and he and his horse flew across the treacherous muddy hazard in one jump. The seventeen-year-old bride knew that this wasn't only good horsemanship; it also showed that her groom of only four hours was as brave as he was good-

looking. Her pride and appreciation of this debonair groom jumped again many degrees. She must have said to herself, *He's mine…my very own.*

He left the affluence of Minnesota

She knew that Gustav had left the affluence of his dad's and mother's several prosperous farms in Minnesota to file on a homestead south of Epping, where he had to face the rigors and uncertainties (another sign of his bravery) of building a small shack and breaking up ten acres of prairie before the US Homestead Act of 1812 would kick in to his benefit. He would then be the owner of 160 acres of virgin soil.

He became the proud owner of this buffalo-grass prairie farm that had not been touched since God's creation or shaken since the Flood. This was actually soil that had never been moved except maybe by a buffalo bull at mating time, digging up the prairie with his powerful pawing feet, or maybe it had been touched by a wandering Native American searching for his dinner of rabbit thighs or buffalo steaks.

From oxen to horses

He remained a proud owner of his land for three years, during which time he owned a team of oxen that he hitched to the plow to do the most strenuous work of breaking up the prairie. He traded them off for two teams of North Dakota wild horses. Taming and training these horses as beasts of burden and for riding became his trademark.

He used this education for making money the next winter, when he would hire out to the large Ford Stockman Garage in Williston. Well, not exactly! It's just that his employer, Mr. Heffernan, and his livery stable were located there in Williston. His winter job took him south to the Little Missouri, the Badlands, Medora, and even as far west as Billings, Montana. Mr. Heffinger and Dad would find wild, untamed horses in Montana, and Dad would herd them back in the fall of the year. During the winter, they would have their own corrals near what is now the bridge across the Little Missouri on Highway 85.

Marriage vows in a tent next to their house (this house is still in the family)

They had time during this ride to talk. She had the ring on her finger and could hear the echo of the sincere spiritual promises they had made only hours before, promises to each other and to their Lord and to the Lutheran Church. Pastor Schlusser, a strong German Lutheran itinerant pastor to the pioneers of western North Dakota, had solemnly impressed upon their minds that this was for life: "Until death do us part." It lasted for sixty years. That promise they had made before God would let nothing— drought, depression, hardships, personal differences, six children, or arguments—separate them from each other or their Lord and the Lutheran Church.

Deep church heritage

Their strong church heritage was embedded in the confessional church. It started when Martin Luther nailed the Ninety-Five Theses onto the Wittenberg Church door in Germany on October 31, 1517. It had its life, vigor, and eternality right from the New and Old Testaments of the Bible. Mother also had this ingrained in her from birth in Germany. Her family followed her brother from Germany to Springbrook, North Dakota. About four years after he left his homeland, her brother became the pastor for the German immigrants in Canada and the Williston area. My uncle was my dad's pastor in the early years.

From Germany to Madison, Minnesota

Dad's mother and father came to the Madison, Minnesota, area from Germany to find a new life and each other in 1880. They were Godfried Hiepler and Henrietta Hiepler and were key people in establishing our dad's home church and fellowship center near Bellingham, Minnesota (we have their marriage certificate hanging in our Heritage Room). He was baptized in this church in 1885 and confirmed in 1898. He and I visited that church and the adjoining cemetery where his parents and other family members were put to rest. This visit was in 1964, shortly before the church was torn down. We were there the day after I went through the trauma of dropping our first daughter off at Concordia College in Moorhead, Minnesota. She was the first one to venture out of our nest at eighteen years old.

They saw stars before nightfall

You can be sure that as they reined their horses close together and looked at each other, their eyes were filled with stars, and their sterling characters radiated optimism, for they were ready for anything. That determination and love followed them all through the good times and adversities of their lives. Their resolves saw them through buying what we know as "our home" from Uncle Henry. They took over his home-stead rights on 160 acres that had failed to produce water.

They had no water for drinking, washing, or watering the horses and cattle. The only way to survive was to haul water three miles from the Hughes Springs. This was a difficult job, both in summer and winter. However, the spirit of "we will make it" always dominated their lives. Daughter Gertrude was born in 1912 and Hildegarde in 1915. That great year of 1915 wasn't only the year of a second daughter being born but also of striking water on the old farm—at 227 feet and at great cost.

This most pleasing string of girls only was interrupted when I was born on February 10, 1920; however, the string was continued when, five years and one day later, on February 11, 1925, Ruth became a part of the happy Hiepler clan. In 1925 times were good, and Ruth received special treatment by being born in the new Good Samaritan Lutheran Hospital in Williston. This good luck of having only girls continued, and Marion arrived on November 23, 1928. Even though this was at the height of pre-Depression good times, Marion was born at home, while Hildegarde and I were hurried off that morning to enjoy the fun of staying with our favorite aunt, uncle, and cousins, the Bartels, just four miles north.

The wonderful string of girls continued during the heart of the Depression, and a wonderful baby arrived on September 9, 1937. This was twenty-four years after Mother gave birth to her first child. Now when the caboose came, Mother almost got to use her name, Anna, as the middle name for Shirley Anne. Dad had succeeded sixteen years previously in preserving his first name for at least another generation when Orville Gustav was born.

Deep, solid Christian anchor
This now became "our home," where we six children lived and grew in wisdom and in the knowledge of the Lord. It was from here that each of us studied the catechism loyally and faithfully and memorized Bible verses in preparation for a personal commitment to Jesus Christ and His church—confirmation day. From Gertrude to Shirley, from

1925 to 1950, we were expected to study with the pastor and then get up in front of the church on confirmation day and answer any questions in the catechism that the pastor might ask of us, all from memory. Florence had the same experience that my family had, except that she remembered everything through the years and I didn't.

If we ever wavered in our faith through the years, this strong grounding gave the Holy Spirit a basis to call us back into a life in His church.

Love and good works dominate

We can picture that happy couple drawing their horses closer together as Gustav leaned over and told Anna in his own way how that shack one-half mile ahead had been pretty lonesome, and now she would make it wonderful. He wasn't the kind to use fancy or colorful words, but Anna already knew him well enough that his kind deeds (for which he was known through his entire life) spoke loads about his love and appreciation.

Throughout their sixty years together, they were most supportive of each other. Differences and even arguments could occasionally be a part of the menu; however, when guests were present, they protected each other, spoke well of each other, and even held the other as an ideal mate. Mom knew Dad was the best farmer and the most daring horseman around. Dad spoke of Anna as the best cook. "Those women from the old country were hard workers," he would say, and Mom would claim that compliment, and then he would playfully say (in his slight German accent), "Yah, you were really too young when you left Germany."

Now they have arrived

I can picture this young couple, with excitement, riding up to their new home together and dismounting from their horses at the barn door, and Gustav saying, "Anna, you stay by the door as I unsaddle the horses and give them some oats and hay."

I can also see this strong, handsome groom carrying his bride across the threshold of that which would become their *castle*.

Five sisters, no brothers—poor me!

Jokingly, I often said that being so small, at only six foot two and 190 pounds, my sisters could easily gang up on me.

Actually, it was just the opposite of "poor me." My two older sisters, Gertrude and Hildegarde, were most helpful and always encouraged me, and from my younger sisters, Ruth, Marion, and Shirley, I have learned to keep up with the times.

What a blessing we four younger children received from our two older sisters. On my first day of school, I rode in a horse and buggy with my older sisters. I grew close to them all through grade school, college, and seminary. Little monetary gifts came to me in college and seminary as they were teaching in the home community. What a surprise for me, and I so appreciated it. My younger sisters all had an older sister as a teacher at one time or another.

I think every family could learn from my parents' wonderful example. We attended church at St. James Lutheran in Springbrook on the days that weather permitted. When the time came that there were more people attending church in Epping and that our church could no longer survive, we made the move to Epping Lutheran. This is where

I was confirmed and served as Luther League president and where I was ordained as a pastor into the Lutheran Church. Throughout their busy lives, my parents instructed their children daily how to live, how to respect one another, and how to make friends and influence others. I suppose as good as it is to read books, go to seminars, and even take classes on how to raise children, it takes more. I believe what my parents did, living life conscientiously by the Golden Rule—"Do unto others as you would have others do unto you"—was the best parenting any child could experience. This is in direct contrast to those who abide by the made-up worldly golden rule, "Those who have the gold rule." My parents provided such a strong and loving environment for their children.

Blizzard tests stamina of new Germans in the United States
Ruth Hiepler Homuth wrote this in 1999, and I thank Ruth's family for the use of this article.

The fate of the Gust Hiepler family would have been different had it not been for my uncle, Reverend Carl Bartels, who came to America as a Lutheran missionary from Germany in 1900. After completing three years of theological training in St. Paul, Minnesota, he was sent to Springbrook, North Dakota, to minister to people throughout Williams County.

The challenges and potential that were offered in this new country gave him reason to encourage his mother and stepfather, Mr. and Mrs. Henry Dreier, and their children—Henry Bartels and Anna, Martha, and Albert Dreier—to immigrate to America. They arrived in Springbrook on March 21, 1906, and filed on a homestead in Marshall Township. Because of the many hardships that faced this pioneer family, Grandpa Dreier entertained desires to return to their good life in Germany, but Grandma Dreier had already attained the true pioneer spirit and decided that they should stay. Even a three-day snow blizzard in November did not discourage her. In fact, after three days of the family huddling around their cook stove in their newly completed four-room house, Grandpa braved the storm to buy a heater at the Henry Graichen hardware store in Springbrook, one of nine other heating stoves sold that day.

In 1908, a young man by name of Gust Hiepler, my father, became the only one of a family of nine children in Madison, Minnesota, to strike out on his own. He left Minnesota planning to file on a claim at Drake, North Dakota, but all the land was claimed, and a traveling missionary assisted him with getting in contact with Reverend Carl Bartels of Springbrook.

Gust Hiepler first worked for Jim McCaan, riding to the Miles City, Montana, area to round up horses and bring them back to Springbrook and Williston. His second job was working for John Heffernan's Transfer and Livery in Williston.

On June 1, 1910, Anna Dreier and Gust Hiepler were married and began farming on the homestead claim, which grew and continued until my father's retirement in 1956. They began their married life in a one-room house and felt very fortunate to be able to add a bedroom built of used lumber two years later, before their first child was born. During harvest my mother baked twelve to fifteen loaves of bread every other day for large threshing crews. One of my dad's specialties was breaking broncos for either riding or as work horses. He broke some of the wildest broncos for Charlie Carpenter of Epping.

My parents devoted much of their time and energy to rearing and educating their six children. They are: Gertrude (Gilmore) Bjella, a grade school teacher who taught in all three Marshall Township schools; Hildegarde (Floyd) Penfield, who has taught for thirty years and is now in Williston public schools; Dr. Orville Hiepler, pastor of Trinity Lutheran Church, Hawthorne, California, who is married to Florence Borstad of Tioga, North Dakota; Ruth (Elroy) Homuth, Annandale, Minnesota, a social worker for the county social service agency; Marion (Daryl)

Bugge, the administrator of a private elementary school in Seattle, Washington; and Shirley (Duane) Syverson, Zahl, North Dakota, who attended business college and held several jobs in the field of business and is now owner of Buffalo Inn Café in Epping.

ES MUSS GEHEN!

If my father, Gustav Adolph Hiepler, could now read the following essay, he would say, "By golly, that's pretty good. I never would have dreamed one hundred years ago that in 2014 my great-grandson, Ryan, would write such an excellent college-application essay on *Es muss gehen!*"

The focus and theme that my dad would demand of his kids has been carried on for at least five generations. "Don't whine or give any excuses; simply get the job done! *Es muss gehen!* (It must go!).

The *Es muss gehen* theme will be carried throughout this book.

Here is the essay written by my grandson Ryan Hiepler:

In my family, the question is: "*Wie geht's?*" (German for "How goes it?"). The correct answer is: "*Es muss gehen!*" (It must go!). Unfortunately, neither the question nor the answer is effectively translated into English because too much context from the original language is lost. To begin, the question "Wie geht's?" carries with it a tone of facetiousness. Until writing this essay, I never wondered why. But I know now that the facetiousness of the question comes because "How goes it?" is a question in simple present form, which is an unusual, old-fashioned way to ask a question. Most questions in English are asked in emphatic present form, such as "How's it going?" or "How does it go?" So, merely asking the question "Wie geht's?" transports the conversation into another, old-fashioned era. Furthermore, the question is facetious because most people really don't want to hear the answer. It is similar to someone today saying, "How are you?" But no one really wants to know how you really are.

They just want you to say, "Well," or "Great, thanks" even if it is a lie. But when my ninety-four-year-old grandfather today asks me "Wie geht's?" he wants and expects only one answer. This is because his underlying question is more accurately translated to something like this: "Son, what would you say if we were two farmers standing on a dirt road with a broken plow and someone asked you, 'Wie geht's?'" My answer, like the generations of stalwart family farmers, attorneys, and teachers faced with difficulties before me, can only be "Es muss gehen!" (It must go!). The answer loses much in translation as well. For the answer is returned also in the simple present form, humorously recognizing the facetiousness of the old-fashioned question, yet replying with the somber message "Es muss gehen!" which means in our family: there are no excuses. I cannot use the weather or any external force as an excuse or to whine about the difficulty I am facing. I must simply stand tall, push my shoulder into the broken plow, and courageously say, "Es muss gehen!" (It must go!). The exclamation point to the answer is essential. In person, the exclamation point can usually be visibly seen with a striking fist pump. It is to say, "Come hell or high water, I shall find a way through sheer determination and elbow grease to overcome this problem."

In my life, the answer, "Es muss gehen!" (It must go!) is often on the tip of my tongue, although I say it out loud only to my grandfather and father. When I get out of school at 3:30 p.m., meet our coach in our home gym for a walk-through, eat a team meal together in the cafeteria, drive an hour or more in traffic to our opponent's school, play in the game as point guard and leave everything I physically have on the court, return an hour or more back to our home campus, then drive 30 minutes to my home, arriving home by 10:00 or 11:00 p.m. with three hours of AP homework still to do before 8:00 a.m. tomorrow, my only option is to say to myself, "Es muss gehen!" (It must go!). It means that I don't have the option to blame my parents for sending me to the most rigorous school in the region, or to blame my teachers for assigning homework on the night of a crucial varsity away game, nor to curse at the traffic (well, OK, sometimes I do that); but still I acknowledge that there is no time to whine or file an excuse, I must simply get the job done because in my family I have learned that "Es muss gehen!" (It must go!). That is the only option.

FROM HORSEPOWER TO TRACTOR POWER

From no telephones to computers
The greatest farming transition happened during my grade-school years. It all began about the time I was born and had changed completely by my college days. What a change it was!

Every farm had a herd of horses numbering from six to sixteen and a tractor of sorts. There was usually one team of two horses and a powerful, sleek saddle horse. Farming changed from putting up hay and raising grain for horse consumption to having to buy gasoline at fifteen to twenty cents a gallon to maintain their one big "iron horse." The countryside changed from having herds of horses out in the open prairie (open range) from October to early April to a few horses for riding or for novelty. Laws were not even written to protect them, so the open range was taken for granted.

If you didn't want horses grazing on your land after the crops were harvested, you would have to fence that land. After harvest, the work horses were turned loose to find their food and graze on the land that was too hilly or too rocky to use for crop land. The horses would usually come home to drink from their regular water tanks until the snow came, at which time they would get their water from the snow and paw their way through the snow to grass. The buffalo prairie grass was known to be rich and healthy for the horses.

The horses were treated well. We knew each horse by name, such as King, Queen, Baldy, Blacky, and even endearing names like Dolly and Girly. How exciting it was when these horses would come home, these wild animals crowding up to the water tank to drink! As soon as they had gorged themselves with water, they were on a fast trot, reveling in their freedom from harnesses and hard work until April. When April came, they would be rounded up, brought back to the barns, and prepared for labor—plowing, cultivating, and seeding that one crop a year, making sure it all got in quickly, as the growing season was short. Here in California we are familiar with land that raises three or four crops a year. What a contrast!

When my dad and mother would come out to visit us in California, another thing that was amazing to them was the size of the farms. My parents couldn't believe what they saw during a California harvest, such as six twenty-foot combines, one after another, going up to four miles an hour, combining hundreds of acres in a day. Just think of the machinery today, all computer set and driven, making the task a "sit back and watch" type of operation. Of course, this is after you master how to work the computerized tractors and combines.

That was such a change compared to the four-horse teams that would pull a reaper or binder. This was followed by a crew of shockers that would pick up the bundles that the binder would form and stack them into rainproof shocks. They needed to be thoroughly dried out for threshing.

The stationary threshing rigs would then wait for the two-horse, one-man bundle racks bringing all of these shocks to be thrown, bundle by bundle, into the threshing machine. Each machine had one blower, out of which came the straw that was next to worthless as far as bringing in any income. The other was a grain spout, out of which golden wheat or whatever grain you were harvesting at the time poured. This grain would produce the paycheck the farmer had worked for and waited for since the last harvest twelve months before.

Which is better, the horse or tractor?
In grade school we had fierce debates on this topic. We had a three-mile-an-hour (top speed) Twin City McCormick Tractor in the late '20s. When I was in fifth grade, my teacher boarded at our house five days a week, so I had the great opportunity to drive her to school. I drove her in a Ford car to our one-room school with ten students. This all changed back to mostly horses because the cost of gasoline was twenty cents a gallon during the '30s. Due to the cost of gasoline, my prestige was diminished when we had to go back to using only the horse and buggy to get to school. Luckily, we children had a great partiality to horses. After all, the horses were some of our best friends! We couldn't at that time ever guess that in less than twenty years we would have the big barns for machinery instead of horses. There really had been very few changes since biblical times until our century with the use of oxen and horses.

By the time I finished college and graduate school, most farms no longer even had a team of horses, which had seemed imperative for the smaller jobs around the farm, such as hauling hay, cleaning the barn, and cultivating the family garden. Even my saddle horse Blacky had died and was not replaced by another horse, because by then they had small tractors to do everything. Tractors did not eat grass or hay and didn't have to be fed when they weren't working! This was so different from the horses. Some farmers who didn't have the open range had to feed their horses all of those months when there was no work. This was especially true in our part of the Midwest, namely western North Dakota, where often the snow began to fall in October and didn't end until March.

Blacky, my favorite horse
He was the fastest horse I had ever seen. He was the quickest horse of all of my friends' horses, especially when I was on him. Blacky was the horse I used in the Great 1934 Cattle Roundup. He made my job of herding cattle and chasing horses almost a pleasure. He was so fast

that he was the favorite horse in the whole community when it came to rounding up the horses each spring. The other horses, after being turned loose in the prairie, acted like wild animals, becoming difficult to corral or be caught. However, Blacky, who was so fast and smart, soon taught them that they had to conform and could not outrun him. They had only one choice, and that was to be corralled.

The last time I ever stood on a galloping horse

It wasn't unusual for a sixth-grade boy at twelve years of age to ride a horse standing up; however, to fall off and get hurt was almost too embarrassing a thing to tell people. I once walked around on crutches for two weeks after a fall. When people asked me what happened, I don't remember if I owned up to the fact that I'd fallen off a horse while galloping or not.

We didn't have big steers to ride, but riding sheep as a small boy was common. Also it was common to ride small yearling bulls of four hundred pounds or so and even cows—around the straw stack, of course, so that when you fell off, it would be a soft landing. These cattle were not wild, so it was easy to jump on them with a little help. No animals liked it, and often they would become startled to have something on their back all of a sudden.

We would ride horse bareback, side saddle, regular saddle, three or four on a horse's back at the same time, and even sitting backward. This made getting the cows from the pasture a little less monotonous and even fun, especially when it happened that there were two of us chasing the cows home. Of my sisters, only the oldest one, Gertie, enjoyed riding horses. Hildegarde was mostly a housebound girl; animals frightened her, especially riding them. The other three sisters were younger. Ruth, five years younger than I, had many other things to do, but she and I did things together when she was older.

My mother, in earlier years, rode horseback with Dad. Dad, as I commented earlier, was a real horseman and always had horses for work and one or more for riding. When I was younger, it was common for

Dad and me to take our two horses and ride together herding other horses or cattle from one pasture to another. Most riding was tied to farming jobs, except when other boys would come over. Some other activities were snaring gophers and taking their tails into town, where we were given a nickel a tail. Big money to us.

The last time I stood up on a horse was plenty scary. I realized after I had fallen rather hard on prairie ground that I couldn't stand on my one foot. I was about a quarter of a mile from home in the back pasture, over a hill where no one would be likely to see me. My little pony, relieved of its rider, had run back home to the barn with the reins dragging. No one at home had even missed me until they saw the pony. They were all busy in their own work and knew I'd make my way. That was just the way life was. I crawled and pulled that one leg along all the way home like anyone would do who couldn't walk, but I was in severe pain. Mother immediately opened our doctor book, a big one, and determined that it wasn't broken, so we never even considered going the twenty miles to see a doctor. She immediately put hot packs on it and told me I could not step on it for a week or two. Even though she had determined it wasn't a break, it was a bad sprain. When it started to swell, it doubled in size and felt even worse than it looked. She found a pair of crutches that I had used during one of my earlier injuries, which kept me from putting any pressure on it.

Mother's doctoring efforts were so successful that less than two weeks later, I was able to throw away the crutches and do almost any normal activity—except for standing on the back of a galloping horse.

No radio or phone

In our farm community in the 1920s, no one had ever used a telephone or even touched one and no one had a radio. When I was in first grade, our neighbor four miles away, Clifford Stewart, purchased a radio, the first in our area. On our way to a Farmers Union meeting, we circled and drove by their farm twice, in awe of someone who had a radio. The Stewarts' stature increased when, a year later, nine of the farm families who had just received a telephone (they were all on the same party line) were invited to lift their telephone receivers at the same time and listen to the W. L. S. Barn Dance Music from Chicago, Illinois. This was a night of entertainment for us! Now in 2014, I hold in the palm of my hand a small gadget that serves as a radio, television, and telephone, plus a camera and computer, and has the ability to contact friends and family in a second. We had the opportunity at Christmas to Skype with our granddaughter, Lisa, and her husband, James, in Perth, Australia. We walked with them through their new home, hearing and seeing everything firsthand as though we were right there with them. To add to that, we even played a game with them via Skype. Another example is a conversation my daughter Dorene had with her two-year-old grandson, William. She told him she would talk with him on the telephone soon, and he said, "No, Grandma, on the computer." This modern technology seems almost unreal when people my age look back at what has happened in our lifetime and what we have experienced. Unbelievable transitions!

Farm life

Every farm child in my day was taught how to do daily chores. It may have been moving large machinery or milking the cows or teaching their calves to drink milk out of a pail. We would entice them with a finger dipped in milk, drawing their heads over and into the pail of milk. That was an accomplishment.

Doing the chores in winter and summer, such as caring for the pigs, calves, chickens, and turkeys and milking the cows was just expected. In addition to that, my sisters and I (at an unbelievably early age) were expected to help with the actual farming, driving the horses, and, in later years, driving the tractor.

The diversification on the farm even affected saddle horses' duties. They became one of a team for winter sledding and light winter farm jobs. I became very fond of the farm animals, especially Blacky, my saddle horse. In the winter, when the roads were often closed to cars because of snow, it was fun to see Blacky and Queen working together.

My father would drive the car, or the horses when needed, seven miles to town every Friday night to pick me up from high school as well as to take me back Sunday afternoons. That seven-mile one-way trip was elongated to ten miles when Dad would pick up my oldest sister, Gertie, a teacher at the Stevens School. Like all of us children, she too always wanted to be home every weekend. In addition to teaching, she and Ruth, one of my younger sisters, lived at the school for five days a week. My parents felt very fortunate that their two oldest daughters, Gertrude and Hildegarde, taught one or more of my three younger sisters, Ruth, Marion, and Shirley. It also saved my dad a considerable amount of driving.

Early morning chores, such as feeding cattle and making sure enough coal was available after a night of rest, were done by my dad. Mom would have breakfast, dinner at noon, and supper to prepare. During harvest, there would be a 4:00 p.m. lunch brought out to the fields. This consisted of meat sandwiches, homemade buns, and nectar in glass jars. Dinner would be much later, as the harvest needed to be done while there was still light. Summer evenings on the prairies were spectacular. Being so far north, we would have light until 11:00 p.m. Wintertime was a little quieter with an earlier supper.

What's this? Prairie boy collecting dry bones?

My granddaughter, Kari, a graphic designer (who created this book's jacket) just said to me, "Papa, include a chapter about the time you collected bones for money during the Great Depression."

Apparently, this made an impression on her. I will share a little background information. It makes some sense when you read the following chapter where a dollar is compared to one hundred dollars today. Also keep in mind that there were crop failures in nine out of ten years in that part of the Midwest in the 1930s. They were often called the "dry and dirty thirties." However, for children and youth, it was still good living. We knew we had enough milk, eggs, and meat to eat. In some years, the garden produced beautiful vegetables, but only if my mother carried water from the house and cattle tank to her garden.

What is an open prairie?

If you'd formed a line five miles directly east and four west from our farm and then four miles north from that line, you wouldn't have found any livable homes. You would have seen some homestead shacks, a few farm places then empty because of the drought and Depression. They had moved to Washington, Oregon, and a few even went to California. Even in good years, you would need more than the original 160 acres given to the homesteaders.

Diversity and hard work were vital factors

During the teens and Roaring Twenties, even people who were experienced were not willing or trained to really diversify with cows, pigs, chickens, and flocks of turkeys. They sold their land to my dad.

My dad had seen at his home farm in Minnesota how a substantial income could be made by raising pigs and other animals. I remember when we had ten brood sows, and some would have up to ten piglets. Pigs grew up in one year and would make a lot of pork for the market in that one year, where cattle would take two or three years to produce good milk cows or large-enough bodies for the beef market.

Open grazing meant horses and cattle found open prairies

The older horses often did not make it during the winter months. Farm horses could break a leg or be injured and weren't worth saving because farming was changing from horses to tractors. I don't remember ever having a veterinarian available on the farm. The farmer knew the Band-Aid type of help. Out of fifty to seventy-five cattle, an occasional cow would also die. I don't ever remember any farmer burying any animal. Cemeteries were for human beings, plus there was that entire open prairie, with its pasture, hills, valleys, and brush. The coyotes and smaller animals needed some food too. The horses and cows had many large bones that no animal could chew; the wild animals would just clean off the meat from them. The hot summer sun, in one or two seasons, would dry up the bones. When herding cattle, or taking them from one pasture to another, we would see where the dead animal carcasses lay. We would take a team of horses on a wagon, or later take a Model T Ford, pick up the bones, and take them into town where they were buying bones as well as scrap iron. They would take the bones and grind them down for calcium.

Old, worn-out farm machinery was often left at the vacated farmhouses for anyone to pick up and make a couple dollars. It wasn't only that we would make a little spending money; it was kind of fun—like a sport for an eleven- or twelve-year-old. We would even snare gophers and bring the tails into town to receive payment. Our parents smiled with approval when we could pick up a few pennies.

On the prairies, when one dollar was equal to one hundred dollars today

On the Midwestern prairies in the middle of the Great Depression in the 1930s, my dad hired men who worked for one dollar a day plus room and board.

In 1937, after a week of Bible camp near Bottineau, North Dakota, in the Turtle Mountains at Lake Metigoshe, I hired out to work at the small farm of a fine Christian man by the name of Oliver Nelson for one dollar a day. I met him at one of our night meetings at Bible camp, when neighbors would come in to hear the speaker of the evening. A dollar a day was great for me. One of the most disliked jobs on the farm was working in the hot, dry, dusty hayfields. Most of it included manual labor, such as pitching the hay into the hayracks in the field and then out of the horse-pulled hayracks into the barn or haystacks. Being familiar with the more open prairies, this area in the Turtle Mountains was surprising to me, situated in the midst of trees, with fields located in clusters where mosquitoes filled the air.

Fruit jar full of pennies

Incidentally, this high-school Bible camp would cost seven dollars for the whole week. Nowadays, it would run a few hundred dollars. The second year in attendance, I surprised the treasurer by doing what he had suggested the year before, which was to save your pennies. I presented to him some fruit jars full of seven hundred pennies. He was really surprised!

Milking cows was better than haying

The ten-hour days were made more pleasant by milking the cows before and after work. Operating the horse-driven mower, rakes, and wagons and pitching hay was very tough work. Ordinarily, to the prairie boy, milking cows wasn't the most glamorous job unless you compared it to haying.

The dollar-a-day rate happened at the peak of the Great Depression. Before then, it had been up to five dollars a day. Today for experienced farmhands, it would be at least twelve dollars an hour or close to one hundred dollars a day for eight hours of work. Prices were decidedly different from today. We sold a dozen eggs for twenty cents and bought a gallon of gas for twenty cents. Postage for letters was two cents and for postcards, a penny. The Lord was good to give us, in the midst of poverty, caring Christian parents. They handled the hardships, and we kids, in most cases, enjoyed the things we had to do.

Perhaps Psalm 79:13 summarizes it: "Then we were people who would praise the Lord forever for generation to generation who will proclaim his name."

SELF-PRESERVATION TAUGHT TO US DAILY

We had heard of more than one person losing his way in a snowstorm, or having a riding horse stumble, and the rider thrown off to be left with scratches and maybe a sprained ankle with no one around for miles to help. We did not know of anyone who had died, thank the Lord. Somehow, people were always found or made their way to safety.

Sickness
Self-preventive cold and flu remedies were numerous. I recall generous amounts of camphor or Vicks rubbed on my neck with a sock wrapped around it. What a smell, but it felt warm. Each child was taught the importance of good eating habits, resting, and safety measures to take. Exercise, also called work, was an everyday necessity.

Keeping healthy was not only important but imperative with doctors twenty miles away. Travel in winter could take a doctor four to five hours. As a very young boy, I remember a man driving a sleigh up to the house. He was a doctor on his way to care for someone another four miles north of our place. His horses were exhausted, and he asked if he could borrow our team and leave his team in our barn until his return. He had traveled twenty-four miles one way.

Weather
We experienced drastic weather changes in that part of the country. It could be 60 degrees on a beautiful fall morning, but by afternoon a full-blown blizzard could take us by surprise. Temperatures varied from 110 degrees in the summer to 58 degrees below zero in the winter. Even in the spring, as late as early June, we could experience an unusual June snowstorm. It was more normal for the frost to be out of the ground and the snow melted by early April so that the seeding of grain could begin in the first weeks of April. The farmer had to hurry and put in long hours seeding because it was well known that the short growing season made practical the saying, "If you can't get the wheat in the ground by May 15, you might as well save it until the next year!" Waiting twelve months meant that you would go for twenty-four months without a check. Living expenses continued as usual.

Fire

The other self-preservation measure we learned was to be careful with fire. Prairie fires could roar across field after field, endangering animals and crop land. A couple of times each winter, a farmhouse would burn to the ground, destroying all the earthly possessions of the occupants. This danger was multiplied many times when you think that our heating, our lighting, and our cooking were done by striking a match. This was true when our lantern in the barn would blow out. The barn was filled with combustible hay and the cattle on which our very existence depended. It meant that at a very early age our parents would scare us half to death by telling us some of the things that happened when kids played with matches or when they pretended or tried smoking out behind a barn. (These cigarettes sometimes would be made from paper or even straw.) Oh, how did I know about smoking behind the barn? It was a common practice in about the fifth grade. Curiosity, you know. The members in our family stayed quite safe, however, thanks to the guidance and daily reminders of my parents.

Lost? No one home? Just walk in!

It wasn't unusual for the doors of our house on the farm to be unlocked. Someone caught in unexpected circumstances could simply come in for shelter during a storm and hunker down there until it was over. I don't think my parents even had a key to the house for many years.

Homesteaders were the first ones to have ever built a shack or house on their land. Previously, the most elaborate dwellings were tents erected by the Native Americans. Depending on the area or the tribe to which they belonged, some would build sod houses or caves under the ground or into the side of a hill.

Neighbors lent a helping hand

Being that it was twenty miles to a doctor or a hospital, people were familiar with serving one another and being dependent on others.

Whether they were only a mile away or farther, it didn't matter. If someone needed help, neighbors and family would come. My grandmother was a midwife, and I remember that my father would take her to the Johnsruds or some other neighbors to help with a birth. It wasn't unusual to spend many days with the family. Someone who was sick could depend on others to help with chores and even do outside work if the man of the house was ill. It was not uncommon in that situation to hear about a farmer's neighbors going to his place and doing all of the spring's work. That meant plowing the ground, cultivating it, and sowing the seed. If there were enough participants, it was possible to do all of the seeding in one day. Sometimes they would have up to four tractors and other farm machinery for that one day. It was a time neighbors and whole families would come together to enjoy a potluck meal and good fellowship. It started out as a hard working day that became a fun occasion for all of the partakers and families. Something very good came out of the bad. That good and helpful spirit affected everyone.

This reminds me of the words that I heard articulated by Robert Schuler: "It is impossible to succeed without helping a lot of people along the way, and conversely you can fail and you will fail, if you do not meet the needs of others."

THE GREAT DEPRESSION

Drought, grasshoppers like a cloud, and armyworms everywhere
Faith, a good work ethic of getting your job done and not expecting or depending upon someone else to do it for you, integrity, and honesty were values instilled in us since birth. Even through the Great Depression, when only one year out of ten in the 1930s did we have any crop to depend upon, we clung to those values. As if crop failure after crop failure, dust bowl storms, and history-making hordes of grasshoppers that would darken the sun weren't enough, we had the crawling army of green worms that could come out and devour any green plants

that were left. We experienced this army of worms a couple of times in 1933 and 1934. They would enter through the smallest cracks as well as open windows, making a home almost unlivable.

Government seed and feed loans made it possible for us to stay on our farm. The interest my parents owed on the seed and feed loan, as well as back taxes owed on the farmland, exceeded what their thousand-acre wheat farm was worth. As a matter of fact, during those days, there was no one foolish enough to ever think of buying farmland. The Federal Land Bank, a government loaning agency, was taking over much of the land in our part of North Dakota because the farmers had not paid on their loans or because the people had left everything and moved on. My parents could see no future in farming and wanted their own children to get an education and not be farmers. This was a bleak time for farmers.

One day they had left—disappeared

The Great Depression separated families. Families left. Even people that appeared to be well anchored in farm life had to leave when tax foreclosures took their land and other jobs were impossible to find in the area. These real hardships had one of two effects upon a family: it tore them all apart, children and parents as well as husbands and wives, or it united them as it did with ours—pulling us all together and, in many instances, helping one another.

My uncle Dan and aunt Martha Brawner lived near to us. Aunt Martha was my mother's only sister. Their children, Delores (my age), Orion, Duane, and Lorna—all under ten years of age—were the closest friends that any ten-year-old could have. I could jump on my little pony anytime and ride up to my cousins' place. (The pony was given to my mother by her mom when they had to move off the old Dreier homestead farm for tax foreclosure.)

Delores had stayed at our home to be closer to school in the first grade, so it was nice to have someone to be in school with as well as to play with. Uncle Dan and my dad worked together frequently, especially at harvest time. Dan would come over and help Dad with the overload of work.

The Brawners and our family were together every holiday and in between, creating such good memories for me.

All of a sudden, they didn't come over; we didn't see them. I had ridden my pony up to their farm, and no one was there. They had disappeared. What a shock to me! Even as I write this section, I have tears flowing down my cheeks, thinking of the loss I felt with them gone.

Because of all of the complications of loans and indebtedness, many people just left without any farewells. My dad would often say that the only ones who stayed on the farm in our area of North Dakota were those who didn't even have enough money to move. There was nothing to do but stay.

Yes, they were all of a sudden gone, and I would not see any of them until after I had finished seminary at age twenty-five. As a ten-year-old, I wondered what had happened, but life went on. I was curious though about some letters scrawled on the side of our old Model T truck. The paint job was much like our school blackboards, rough and porous, so the letters and words about a town in Illinois were stained into the back part of the vehicle and lasted there for years. What I later found out was that before leaving, my uncle had scratched down his uncle's address in Pawnee, Illinois. He had been offered a carpenter job by his uncle. If you were ever offered a job, you needed to jump at that chance. That showed he had love, ambition, and concern for his family's well-being.

Before settling down, I traveled to Pawnee, Illinois, to see my dear cousins and family. By this time, all of the children were married; little Orion had died from a gun accident when he was still in grade school. All of the children lived near their parents' home, so when I came for a visit, it was a great reunion! What a time of reminiscing!

Through the years, we understood that Uncle Dan had gotten a job as a carpenter working with his brother. We knew that they had bought their own house and, above all, that they had had a new spiritual experience and were very active in their church. Their daughter, Lorna, married a man who became a pastor. I was only back to Pawnee once with Florence, Dorene, and Ilene and then a few years ago when my precious cousin Delores had passed on to heaven. In years past, many from the Brawner family had come back to North Dakota for a visit and for my parents' anniversary. Aunt Martha (as a widow) had spent some summers with my parents in Williston.

Some unbelievable sadness during the Depression years! Were these really "the good old days"?

INORDINATE INFLUENCE OF TWO "OLD" BACHELORS

The inordinate influence of two old bachelors, Rudolph Haakinson and Haakon Johnson, on me was most unusual because they both had become almost hermits; they weren't jokesters, funny, or athletic. Sports and national leagues were not topics of discussion in our small country community. The biggest concern of these two men was eking out a living on their very small farm. Many farms were too small for dry-land farming, and many still only used horses.

Rudolph was more like an older uncle to us, and Haakon filled the role of an independent yet caring grandfather. One lived less than a half mile east of us, and the other lived the same distance south of our home farm. We would see these two men more than anyone else.

Our other neighbors, two miles east and then four miles north, were my aunt and uncle. In the deep winter snow and blinding snowstorms, we made trips to these homes less frequently.

These two men did not go to any church. One never owned a car, and the other bought a 1929 Model A for his first auto. A couple years earlier, he had purchased the smallest tractor made by Ford Motors, called a Fordson. My dad's larger tractor could pull a three-bottom plow, and this little tractor seemed to grunt at even the smallest pile of dirt.

When Haakon Johnson quit farming and wanted to employ Carl Erickson, the well-known auctioneer in our community, to come and have his sale, whom did he ask to take him to the town of Springbrook five miles away to confirm the sale? He asked me, inasmuch as he had seen me driving around the farm and to school. (At only ten years old, by the way.) So with permission from my parents, I drove the car with Haakon as my passenger, to firm up the sale.

Daily we would see Haakon Johnson walking the road across the small field from our house to the mailboxes down on the corner. I would often run over and stop him so that we could have a talk. He walked with a cane, as he had had a runaway with his team of horses a few years before. Even though he was only sixty years old, he walked with a limp like an old man, as he had never gotten his leg fixed properly. He seemed old to a ten-year-old. A few times, he walked across the field and up to our house to visit with Mom and Dad while they were outside working on machinery or gardening. When I herded our cattle up past his house to a better pasture, he would sometimes come out to talk. My parents would always have the answer as to why it took me so long: "Oh, I bet he was talking to Haakon again." They would say this with a smile, of course.

May Day—fun times!

May Day was a fun time for farm children. Baskets were filled with goodies that Mom had baked. Mother was one of the best cooks and bakers of anyone around. We would run over to Rudolph's or to Haakon's with our baskets, knock on the door, and run away. Most of the time we would let them catch us, as they would have candy for us. These men were like family and would join us at Christmas and Easter. They admired my dad for finding a wife and not waiting until everything was perfect and for having a family of six children even when the savings account wasn't much.

Even though these men were not German or Norwegian and didn't go to a German or Norwegian Lutheran Church (the main churches in our community), they lived lives that were great examples for us children. They were Swedish and had no Swedish-speaking church near unless they went twenty miles to Williston. It wasn't until the late '30s that a church service was held in the Swedish language in our community. Why were their moral values and way of life so sanctified? Thinking about this now, I credit it to their families, the way they were raised, and being a part of a great spiritual renewal in Sweden during the middle 1880s. Some came to this country as Swedish Baptists and some as Swedish Lutherans. Socially, they were very straightforward and strict. This was very similar to the Old Norwegian Hauge synod from which some of our pastors came who would caution us concerning social matters. Rudolph and Haakon were role models to me as well as truly part of our family.

MOTHER TRUSTS A FOURTEEN-YEAR-OLD DRIVER

It occurred to me as I was driving my rental car back from Tioga to Minot, North Dakota, in June of 2014 that this sleek four-lane, two-way highway wasn't always like this. The cloudy, rainy weather was very mild compared to something that came to mind from many years ago. That episode was in the fall of the year, when the weather was unpredictable. When I stopped near Stanley, North Dakota, to pick up some Wheat Thins and a Coke so that I would stay awake on the road after a very intense weekend of speaking, I recalled that we didn't even have any service stations on that highway eighty years ago. At least they wouldn't have been open after dark at that time of the year on this very same road, which is now a four-lane divided highway.

Dad left behind

Our trip of 120 miles eighty years earlier had been for the purpose of visiting Dr. McCannel, a well-known eye doctor. My dad had seen him previously for some eye problems; however, this time was different because he was to have surgery on one eye for cataracts. In those days, you had to stay in the hospital for over a week after cataract surgery. During that time, you were not permitted to turn to either side, so you had to sleep on your back and keep the eye covered for at least seven days. Any sudden movement, shake of the head, or a quick change in your head's upright position would endanger the success of the whole surgery.

Our home away from home
Mother and I remained in Minot until the surgery was successfully completed. Most likely we had stayed overnight for only two days with our former depot-agent friends from Springbrook, the Retzloffs, who were friends of my parents from their single days before my parents were married in 1910.

My parents had anticipated that Dad would not be able to come back with us because of the seriousness of the surgery. Therefore, I would be the driver for the return trip home, and apparently, this was no problem because I had been driving around our neighborhood for a few years. However, they never planned on bad weather and that we would be driving in rain, sleet, and a snowstorm.

My mother would not even touch the controls of a car after her accident in Springbrook when I was only four years old and riding in the car with her. The accident involved a Model T Ford touring car with curtains and all the rest. Mother took a little pride in saying that after that accident, she would never even pretend to have anything to do with driving again. She always took good care of us children and left the driving to someone else.

Slipping and sliding sideways and traveling very slowly changed the usual two-and-a-half-hour trip into a torturous five-hour drive, making it long after dark before we reached our home.

The only car on the road
This time, when we were taking a trip in our old 1926 Chevy, I was the driver. I was familiar with the car, and Mom felt comfortable with me behind the wheel driving the family back home. Two of my younger sisters were also with us on that trip. No one expected such inclement weather or that the windshield wipers wouldn't work in the freezing

rain and snow. The horrible weather started shortly after we left Minot. After the first hour of driving, we were the only car on the road.

No stopping overnight at a hotel

In those days you would never think of stopping overnight at a hotel, even if one was available. First, there was the cost factor, as this was right in the midst of the '30s Depression. Second, we had chores to do, such as milking the cows and caring for the chickens and the hogs. Most likely a neighbor would have helped out during a time of illness and would thus have taken care of the first two days, but we were expected back that night, so the animals were wholly dependent upon us. Mom and I were concerned about the girls becoming too cold also. Back then, everyone carried heavy horse blankets in the cars, so we bundled the girls up in the backseat. There was no thought of not getting home. After about ten miles, the windshield was so absolutely filled with snow and ice that I couldn't see through the glass. So guess what? I, the fourteen-year-old driver, would stop and get out in the freezing temperature, using some makeshift kind of scraper to clear the windshield and thus restore visibility. I would then jump back into the car, but this jumping in and out every so often would let that cold northwest wind into the car, so we were constantly checking that the girls in the backseat were OK.

My hands would hardly get warm before we had to stop once again and clear the windshield. Even though Mother was busy with the girls, I felt in charge, as she was always so thankful for what I did and how I never gave up. The good thing was that Dad didn't know anything about this until it was all over. After many stops and five hours of slowly making our way back, we finally arrived home.

This incident was among many that helped develop responsibility, perseverance, and a sense of accomplishment in me. I wanted to see my job through until it was completed. Getting everyone safely home was my goal. It seemed very commonplace to me at that time. It would be what any ordinary man would do. *Es muss gehen!*

When we arrived at home safely, we were thankful that we had not landed in the ditch and that we were out of the storm. Now we could all thaw out in the safety of our house. We did have to hurry to the barn, milk the cows, feed the animals, collect the eggs, and get the chores completed before our day came to an end. If we hadn't warmed up before then, doing the chores took care of that.

THE GREAT WILLIAMS COUNTY ROUNDUP OF 1934

Ten young farm boys, I being the youngest at fourteen years of age, would be real western cowboys for a few days! Riding our farm horses, we rounded up and herded five hundred head of cattle for twenty miles in two days to the stockyards in Williston, North Dakota. Years later we would talk about and relive this exciting adventure many times.

We looked forward to the anticipated harvest, but to have this exciting roundup was a first for me. Getting the cattle to the staging or gathering area of the stockyard in Williston was a bit awesome, as the area usually accommodated up to sixty head of cattle. Our contribution of five hundred head was about the largest ever for this stockyard. After arriving at the stockyards, the cattle were sent to be slaughtered in St. Paul, Minnesota, and used for food.

We farm children became close to our animals, even though marketing a few was expected and was needed for income. Each of us would-be cowboys, as well as our parents, would have touches of emotion when the time for taking them to the stockyards would come. We were chasing our milk cows and calves away from their homes, and we would never see them again. Most of the young stock we had been with since they were born; however this roundup was a godsend, as the government would buy them, and we needed the income.

Some of the farmers would keep their big two-year-old steers, as they were optimistic and always thinking that the prices would go up.

Now they faced a crisis: each farmer was up against something he had never known—*no* price, *no one* buying, and *everyone* cutting back.

This forced them to make decisions about the cattle. They would keep what they needed for their family and then take the rest of the cattle to the coulee and shoot them. The government would buy the large cows and steers from the farmer for twenty dollars a head and the calves for seven dollars a head. The farmers were used to getting at least four times more for the cattle than this, but it did give them a little financial relief.

The Great Roundup of 1934 and some other firsts

There was no immediate family nearby. I had never slept outside under the stars with neither walls around me nor a roof over my head. It was necessary because we had to be alert to make sure none of the cattle would break through Earl Swimley's corral fence and head back home. We also had each of our saddle horses staked out right near our sleeping spot in case we needed to jump on and head off some cattle trying to go back home.

Morning sunlight was welcome, and the large cowboy breakfast tasted *so* good!

Never had I been faced with so many unknowns in a day. How long would it take to herd five hundred cattle? Would the weather stay dry? Would my horse Blacky do OK? How long would we be gone?

We proudly herded the cattle to the stockyards within a couple of days, and all went well. We returned home after the task was completed. I was honored to use my horsemanship as my dad, a great horseman, had taught me. I felt so pleased to be able to be a part of this endeavor at age fourteen.

What did the farmer have left after this, you ask?

Usually their beef herd and their milking cows were cut back to the very minimum. This was the end of summer, and the growing season was coming to an end. Most of the hay and feed for the cattle, horses, and pigs had to be shipped in and paid for with money that would come from feed loans from the government.

The farmers kept enough cows for home use, also for making a little income from the cream that was sold to make butter, while the skim milk would be fed to the pigs.

In spite of the unbelievable hardships of the Depression, the sixteen-hour workdays in the summer and next to no income for years, we were blessed. Those of us on the farm had our milk, eggs, butter, and meat, while the people in town usually did not have any way of getting these provisions. Yes, being a farmer during the Depression was not such a bad thing (from the perspective of a fourteen-year-old boy).

PHENOMENAL CROP FAILURE AND THE GREAT DEPRESSION DON'T LAST

Phenomenal faith does
As a youth growing up in the "dirty thirties," I can't remember even one time when I didn't know that things were soon going to be better. My parents had faith that it could only get better. However, in my personal life, I had some unbelievable disappointments with illness on my fourteenth and fifteenth birthdays.

I spent my fourteenth birthday in bed with a serious case of measles followed by weeks of illness, and I also spent my fifteenth birthday in the hospital. This was the first time I had ever been in a hospital, as I was born at home. I had an appendectomy and six months of disability followed by anemia, Saint Vitus dance, and overall weakness and nervous exhaustion. This was strange, for most people saw me before and after as a most agile, strong, well adjusted, athletically inclined hard worker from sunup to sundown in farm work or other work activities. This was unbelievable! When my farm neighbor friends would come and visit me (I was in the Williston hospital twenty miles away), they would leave feeling helpless, as there was nothing they could do for me. But when friends came to visit and brought the delight of any boy, delicious ice-cream sundaes, I never had a thought of feeling sorry for myself. I felt guilty that I was drawing all of this attention and that I couldn't be home helping with the overabundance of work that was now all on my precious father's and mother's shoulders.

My birthday is in February, wintertime, when most major farm work is dormant. My parents, being industrious German farmers, had a diversified farm. There was the feeding of the pigs, chickens, sheep, and horses and all of the accompanying jobs. Our farm was not modern with running water to the barn or the house unless you took the pail and ran with it from the well to the house. On stormy days, we had to figure out how to get water to the seventy head of cattle and a team of horses in the barn when the stock couldn't even get it out of the water tank. We also had to haul hay from the stacks out in the field, placing it into hayracks pulled by a team of horses, to the front door of the barn and then pitch it up into the haymow, which was the second story of the barn. Twice a day we would then drop the hay, as needed, down through holes into the manger below for the horses and cows to eat. I was not able to help and do my part.

In order to keep the barn clean in the winter because of the extra amount of manure, we cleaned it daily, and weather permitting, we would load it into a spreader pulled by horses and spread it in the fields or on top of the snow for fertilizer for the next summer's crop. Faithful fertilizing of the ground would produce a better crop the next year. I was not able to do my part.

Guilt raged in me as I watched my dad outside working so hard while I was housebound. This feeling was multiplied when spring work came, when I usually was eager to work in the field so we could enjoy the coming harvest. In 1935, we yielded the only good crop we had for some time, and I was looking forward to replacing a hired man. Now I was fifteen years old and expected to do a man's work, and I had been well trained. Dad had as much confidence in me as in a full-grown, trained, hired worker. I would be able to be the sole tractor handler or even perform the more technical job of running the grain-reaping combine. It was a thrill for every farm boy to reach that place in life. It really wasn't work, but great prestige was connected to this position, and I was not able to do my part.

Help from son? No, the opposite happened!

In the summer of 1935, when my parents expected to get some relief from their work because they finally had a homegrown, full-time harvest-worker son, they were instead concerned about finding the right doctor for me. I wasn't able to do any hard work, and all farm work was just that—physical labor.

The worst thing in the eyes of a fifteen-year-old was that I was unable to be out running the combine or tractor like the rest of the men. I wouldn't hear the compliments my mom and sisters would make when bringing out lunch to the workers at 4:00 p.m. ("Isn't Orville doing a good job, and he's only a little more than a kid"), or comments from the neighbors, who would be so surprised that I was so well trained and could run the machinery by myself. I missed all of this and was unable to do my part.

Harvesting

I should add, too, that it was fun and satisfying to feel well trained to do the men's jobs and to be able to do something as important and worthwhile as harvesting. This was a very time-consuming job and needed to be finished within a certain time frame. The women would have to bring the noon meal (dinner) out to the working men. No time off to go home and eat, even though it may have been within four miles of home. Distances depended upon whether you were harvesting on the west eighty or on the quarter (160 acres) four miles away. Time was of the essence!

When the women came with the meal, the workers would take about a twenty-minute break and then hurry back to start the tractor or combine and go for a round or two. The women would watch and then be on their way. As the combine roared on, the straw came out of the back of the combine and would be spread out on the ground as a little fertilizer for the following year, while the most valuable kernels of golden wheat dropped into the highest spot on the machine called the hopper, which in those days would hold about forty bushels. The truck driver or the horse-drawn grain wagon would pull up under the hopper for about a five-minute fill-up stop. When completed, the rig would immediately pull out, and again you could see those golden grains of wheat now dropping into an empty tank until another round, when it would be full again. You would have the same routine until the truck was full. The grain truck would then hurry away to the granary and would return empty waiting for the next load.

All of this excitement and work was done to get the one paycheck a year every farmer depended upon. Of course, if there was crop failure, there would be no check for twenty-four months.

These motives made it such an exciting time, *and I was missing it all*!

On top of it all, my wonderful parents took time (at this most busy time of the year) to check out a new sort of miracle-working doctor located in Hanks, North Dakota, even farther and in the opposite direction from the twenty miles to our regular doctor in Williston. Some called this man a quack. He had moved into an old, unused building in this small town where no one would start a practice unless he couldn't find any other place. Even at that time, very few would think of him as a licensed professional. As I look back after eighty years, I'm convinced even more that the Lord had guided my parents to do this extraordinary thing because they were perplexed about what to do for me and would do anything that was possibly worthwhile.

This doctor was what we would call a holistic doctor with some chiropractic knowledge. He perhaps didn't have the credentials, even in that day, to get into a clinic; however, I credit him (and God working through him) for giving me exactly what I needed. My body responded very well to the light massage and adjustments and to his quiet, confident concern for my whole person. He taught me how to relax; I use that knowledge to this day when I can't sleep. I start telling each part of my body, beginning with my ears and nose, to relax. Usually, by the time I get to my toes, I am asleep. He realized that my family, my church, and others had taught me well, but that I needed some suggestions from an outside source to help me get through these tough times. The book of Obadiah emphasizes the importance of dealing with yourself and others. This fine doctor, after some time of counsel and treatments, knew that my worries were much more than I needed or should have had to endure.

I was affected abnormally by little disagreements among members of our family, even my parents. I continually felt a great amount of guilt because I could not be out there helping my dad and contribute to the livelihood of our whole family. I had weird thoughts of what might happen. I had no self-esteem. I realized later that these concerns weren't as important as I had thought at the time. This doctor caught all of this. The physical therapy and the counseling couldn't have been any better for me.

I was out of step and missed it all

I had missed the first-semester final in January when I was sick. I realized that finals were not easy when you are out of step with your class. During the summer months, when I was not able to do the physical farm work, I made up the finals for the second semester that I'd missed. Mr. Fossum, our school superintendent, invited me to make up the semester at his home in Epping. What a wonderful, dedicated man to use a few days of his summer for me!

With the doctor's help, in a matter of weeks I was able to face all of these things with a healed body, mind, and soul. When September came along, I was back in school, had completed my semester exams reasonably well, started trombone lessons, played in a second band, and began to look forward to the Band Days in Williston the following spring. Not only would I be able to attend Band Days, but I would be able to march, playing my trombone with the best of them. I started going out for basketball and improved considerably in only months. Thanks to Mr. Rosenquist, I also enrolled in an after-school credited course of Old Testament Bible. About that time, I became a minor officer in our church youth group called the Luther League. I met with the student leaders and the principal at our school, as he was our adult advisor.

Above all, now, at the start of my junior year, I could go home and work from early to late with my dad on Saturdays. Sometimes my dad would have me skip a day of school when he had some pressing jobs to get done. Work was, at times, more important than school.

We had faith that things would get better, and they did.

To this day, I thank the Lord for the rather unorthodox doctor who knew exactly what I needed. My parents had built a firm foundation, with God's help, from which the doctor could build.

After good crops in 1935, my parents could afford sixteen dollars a month room and board for me at our friends, the Beachlors. Mr. Beachlor was the hardware store owner, and his wife became like a second mother to me and remained so as long as she lived. That was a great contrast to living with Lelland Christopherson in an old granary during my freshman year. The Christophersons and my dad had moved the building, which had a single interior wall, no insulation, and no storm windows, into town onto a vacant lot. We spent the weekdays and nights there and even did our own cooking, if you could call it that. That was our home during the week, as the seven-mile drive home was too difficult to do every day. We were so thankful for what our dads had done. Some country kids had to stay home and not attend school.

I never looked back on my illness in high school. It was a good experience of finally good health and good grades and of actually making the starting basketball team my senior year. When I attended Grandview, a one-room grade school, we'd play baseball, so I hadn't touched a basketball until high school. I was selected as one of the top ten players out of the ten teams in the first tournament in our district. I think I happened to play my best in my last high-school game—not the championship game but what was known as a consolation game, determining who would be third and fourth place.

Probably one of the most important things that could have happened to someone like me was to be elected president of our Luther

League at our church in Epping. We met every third week, and it was for the entire church to attend. Those Sundays I became almost sick to my stomach thinking about standing in front of the whole congregation and leading the whole meeting, but I did it. *Es muss gehen!* (It must go!). Everyone was very tolerant and gave me encouragement, even though I knew I didn't do a good job. This opportunity gave me the encouragement and strength for what God had planned for me in the future. I also had the opportunity before harvest time in 1937 to hop in the back of a pickup truck with others from our community and attend camp at Lake Metigoshe. This is where my life changed, and I received a nudging from the Lord to enter the ministry.

It could be summed up in the words from Hebrews 13:5–6a: "God will never leave you nor forsake you so that you may boldly say, 'The Lord is my helper and I will not fear.'"

COLLEGE THEN AND NOW

Dorene, granddaughter Rachel, and myself at Concordia

Peculiar, strange, or unbelievable facts from college days
The following items point out the contrasts between what I did seventy-six years ago to what my grandchildren do today.

1. No one would think of calling home to chat. There was one pay phone in our entire men's dorm, and it cost money to call long distance. This was at a time when a penny postcard or a two-cent stamp on a letter was cheaper. I recall only one long-distance call during my four years of college, and that was when my sister Ruth was seriously ill and not expected to live. I needed to go home immediately. I managed to hitch a ride all the way home and arrived there sooner than I would have if I'd waited for the train. (Ruth did recover.)

2. All of the guys in our dorm would send their dirty clothes home in a little mailer box every ten days for their mothers to wash and return. How often did I wear a pair of underwear?

3. I had only two to three trousers and would place them under my mattress to press. I had one good pant-and-shirt outfit for Sunday wear and one for work.

4. Only one student out of five hundred had a car at our school. We walked almost everywhere, even over to the neighboring town, Fargo, which was across the river. Buses cost money, and shoe leather was cheaper. My friend Ed Leivestad loved to walk and would take dates on walks. One night he and his date had walked for two hours, and she was tired out. Ed took her back to Fjelstad Hall and then asked her if she knew of any other girl that would like to go out walking.

5. Many of us were allotted government aid called National Youth Administration, a work-study training program for students. I worked for twenty cents an hour.

6. Our tuition was seventy-five dollars a semester in a very highly academic Christian college.

7. There was no dancing on campus.

8. Pool halls were off limits because they were known more as hangouts for "low- lifers."
9. Entertainment was attending plays, in which I also participated. I was in Alpha Psi Omega Society and in three plays my first year. (I almost flunked out of school!) Choir and band concerts were highlights of the year. Daily chapel was required and, of course, Sunday church services.

College was such a memorable four years of my life. My Christian life grew due to the nurturing of teachers and pastors. I started lifelong friendships, which have meant so much to me and my family. One example is my dear friend Ed Astrup. After graduation we would get together through the years to discuss (but not always agree on) theological matters or what was happening in the world. Our families would visit each other either in North Dakota or California and share enjoyable times. His son David and our daughter Dorene were the same age and were classmates twenty-five years later at Concordia. When our granddaughter Rachel was a student at Concordia, she would even visit Ed at his home in Moorhead and developed a wonderful relationship with my friend. At this time in 2014, Rachel and Ed's daughter, also named Rachel, served together on the National Alumni Board of Concordia and have since become great friends. So many connections! What great friendships developed through the years because of my wonderful alma mater, Concordia College of Moorhead, Minnesota.

HITCHHIKING

"Jump in; I'm on my way to heaven!"
There is no limit to the extraordinary experience of a person hitchhiking a ride on our roadways, and we did this often in college. It was unfortunate if you hadn't gotten a ride by the time darkness set in, or if you had to stay overnight in a strange town when you didn't have

enough money for a room. This was even worse if it was winter on the prairies of North Dakota.

All of these negative aspects were present at the same time when my college friend Lloyd Larson and I decided to hitchhike home from college in Moorhead, Minnesota, for a holiday—a four-hundred-mile trip. We had gotten a ride as far as Minot, North Dakota, 120 miles from Williston. Thinking that the next leg of our journey would be easy, and looking forward to our warm, cozy houses, homemade foods, and lots of love, we didn't realize our bad timing—darkness had set in, which meant less traffic. We found the lobby of a hotel that was warm and comfortable in which to sit and wait out the nighttime hours. About midnight, the night clerk made it clear that no one could stay overnight in the hotel without getting a room. The lobby was off limits. A little after midnight, walking the streets, we noticed a Ford dealership with some lights on, and we got the night watchman's attention. He was our angel. He very generously said we both should come in from the cold, and he let us into the main office of the garage. He suggested that we sleep in the new Ford 8 on the display floor. We liked the smell of the new car and especially the warmth inside.

We were up and out early in the morning with no breakfast and in eager anticipation of getting a ride to our homes 120 miles away. We had visions of our moms' farm tables heaped high with good vegetables, meat, and even pie.

Even in the morning light, traffic was sparse and especially lacked anyone traveling over one hundred miles. There was a general rule among hitchhikers that you did not want to accept a ride with anyone going only to the next town or only partway. The other well-known practice was to try to catch a ride in a newer car because it would go faster and be safer.

After less than a perfect night of sleep and conditions on the road looking bleak, our attention was suddenly drawn to a rickety, noisy older car coming down the road. Before we could turn our backs with disinterest, we saw and heard the noisy car slowing up and a young man's kind voice yelling, "Jump in, I'm on my way to heaven!" Of course our immediate thought was that we did not want to go to heaven today, but he *was* traveling the 120 miles we needed to reach home, so we laid aside all of our fears and hitchhiking ethics, smiled, and said, "Thank you, and we're happy to go with you!"

We hadn't been home since we left for college in August, so you can imagine how we felt when we arrived at our homes with all of the welcoming any college guy would love. The best things were the great food, a lot of conversation, gifts, warm beds, and the precious love that only a family can give.

My parents and the Larsons didn't want us hitchhiking back to college, so they managed to scrape together enough money for a train ride back to school after two weeks of vacation.

I RISKED ALMOST FREEZING TO DEATH

I wanted to avoid doing anything that could be taken as wrong. Florence and I were so well respected as high-school and college students, as well as the two years after college, that we wanted everyone to think that we were very careful and appropriate during our courtship. Wintertime is the coldest time on the prairies of North Dakota, especially in January. This was right before we were engaged in February of 1945. I would go through any snowbanks, storms, or cold weather just to be with her, as I felt in her presence a most wonderful relationship was developing during this period of our lives. At the age of twenty-four I was seriously thinking about a life mate, and Florence was analyzing the whole relationship and realizing this was more than just dating.

Both of us had dated some in high school and college; however, this was different. It was serious. During that Christmas vacation, I just wanted to be with her as much as possible. The fact that I had six more weeks of seminary before I would see her again when I came home for my ordination on February 24 may have increased my desire to be with her. I realized I wouldn't be able to see her until then, even though we did write to each other almost every other day during those six weeks. I tried to convince her to come to St. Paul, Minnesota, for my graduation. She wanted to come, but her schedule would not permit it, plus I think her desire to behave ethically during the courtship may have entered into the picture of staying in St. Paul for two or three days before she was married. We were dating seriously, but her reasoning was that we weren't even engaged at this point, and she had been taught not to be too anxious until you knew for sure that this guy was "the one." (Hint: Why don't you propose?)

My parents, who didn't travel much, came the six hundred miles to the graduation in February. My uncle Carl and aunt Pauline came from West Union, Iowa, where Uncle Carl was a pastor. I had only seen my uncle and aunt a handful of times in all my life. It was most kind and even unexpected for them to come to my seminary graduation. However, in spite of those two important couples coming, I would have been more thrilled if Florence had surprised me and come to Minnesota. By this time, I was sure she was "the" girl. She, however, may not have been as sure.

What has seminary, graduation, and all this to do with my almost freezing to death? That may be putting it a little too strongly, but I really don't know of any other time in my life when I was colder than that night.

On that date during Christmas vacation, we stayed at home and got better acquainted with each other because our courtship wasn't even one year old. We had met a couple of times before, and I knew her as a teacher with my sister Hildegarde in Tioga. Also, Floyd, my brother-in-law, was her superintendent and had become good friends with Florence.

First meetings with Florence
I met Florence during a community celebration at a meeting on the Fourth of July at the Epping-Springbrook Dam and again at a meeting in Ray, North Dakota. Florence came there with her hosts while

teaching vacation Bible school in Temple, North Dakota. My host while I taught vacation Bible school in Wheelock, North Dakota, invited me to go with them to this same celebration and tent meeting.

Incidentally, the dam, forming a beautiful lake, is where they started a Bible camp a few years later. (Now it is the beautiful Upper Missouri Bible Camp with year-round camping. That is where I had been invited to speak for three days in August 2014.) I also knew Florence's cousins and had been at their home across Highway 40 from Florence's farm home. As a matter of fact, my best friend from high school dated Florence's cousin, Gladys. I also had gone to college at Concordia College in Moorhead, Minnesota, for one year with both Gladys and Bob Borstad. They were seniors when I was a freshman. Gladys was a beautiful singer in the Concordia choir as was Florence in the Augsburg choir.

The night I asked Florence for a date was so cold, maybe reaching thirty degrees below zero, that we decided to stay inside at her home. I was eager to visit with her parents. I didn't know them, but after hearing such good things about them from their relatives, it was a pleasure to get to know them both. After 10:30 p.m., Florence's parents went to bed. Spending time with Florence and her parents was so important to me.

About midnight, I suggested I had better go home because my farmer parents would be getting up early the next morning for milking cows, and I always helped when I was home. She didn't give any indication of asking me to spend the night, even though they had at least five bedrooms in their nice, large farmhouse. But I had grabbed my overnight kit just in case I was asked to stay with her family.

More wonderful each time I saw her

Florence was so nice to get all bundled up to walk with me to my car in the blustery, cold, and stinging wind to see me off. As she recalled years later, it never even entered her mind to have me stay over. It just wasn't the proper thing to do. So off I went. I waved and waved and blinked my car lights, hoping she would note every indication of a person who really loved her.

Frightening drive with a killing northwest wind

What a miserably cold night. Almost eight miles out toward my home fifty miles away, and four miles past the town of Tioga, my car was all steamed up, and smoke was coming out of the motor. I knew from frequent experience what was happening. I'd left the car too long outside and had not warmed it up all evening. The mixture of Prestone and water-freezing deterrent was not strong enough in my parents' car in this severe cold. The radiator was not strong enough to keep ice from forming in the radiator's tubes; thus all of the water remaining had steamed and boiled out. So in my light clothes, which I would not have ordinarily worn in this weather but did so because I wanted to leave a nice impression on Florence's parents, I stopped at the first possible farmhouse. It was 12:30 a.m. when I pounded at the door. After about five minutes of standing on their doorstep, almost frozen, the farmer came to the door in his nightclothes, welcomed me in, and asked if he could help me. He knew that, ordinarily, no person in his right mind would be out in that kind of weather, especially past midnight.

He knew what to do and heated water over his stove. He and I ventured outside and poured the radiator full of warm water from his teakettle, and everything began to run again. I needed to keep the car warmed up and running constantly. If my parents had had a heated garage, there would have been no problem, or if the barn had been empty, I could have parked there, but it was completely full of livestock on such a cold night. I had no place to put the car, except in a totally unheated place, which I could not do now. With most of the Prestone steamed or boiled out, I had mostly pure water, which would immediately freeze once I turned off the car. I was now very concerned that if I continued on home, I would get a cracked block, meaning that the entire block or main part of the cooling system in my motor would actually burst when the water froze.

I was left with only one choice: return to Tioga and awaken my sister and brother-in-law. They lived in the basement of the school and would have to be awakened some way. This was my next task. I went to the smaller windows partly under the level of the first floor and banged at almost every window, all around that big school building. During this time, I was getting colder and colder. I couldn't think of being tired and wanting to go to sleep; if you do when you become that cold, you fall asleep never to awaken again.

All of a sudden, a shade was pulled up, and I saw two people starring out at me with a look of surprise and then disgust, when they saw that it was I who had awakened them. Hildegarde thought I should have known better than to be out in this terrible weather. But they knew how to call the night serviceman at the Ford garage. The actual owner answered the phone, and as he would do almost anything for the school superintendent, especially in an emergency, I was able to park my car in the warm garage.

Floyd and Hildegarde were more than happy to thaw me out and give me their guest room for the night. This night's activities gave all of us—Florence, myself, Hildegarde, and Floyd—something to talk about and laugh about through the years. In the words of the immortal Shakespeare, "All's well that ends well."

PRAYERS ANSWERED—YES, NO, OR WAIT?

It almost kept me out of the ministry. When I was in junior high, my confirmation pastor had asked me not to sing but to mouth the words to a song. When you are told you aren't good at something by one of authority, you presume it is true. So I took piano and voice lessons during college. I did get into the second choir at Concordia College by virtue of my voice teacher, who was the director. My lack of confidence and ability caused me to shudder even in teaching Bible school and then, of course, even when trying to start the table grace song. While teaching vacation Bible school in Springbrook, Wheelock, and Epping, and especially in my intern work in Parshall, North Dakota, I had no confidence in using my "poor" vocal abilities. God didn't seem to give me the help I prayed for, even during my second year at seminary. "No" and "wait" were the answers I received.

Praise to the Lord, alleluia—the answer came

The summer before my last semester at the seminary and only six months before graduation, the Lord finally answered, "Yes." The answer came in part through my sister Hildegarde and her husband, Floyd, the teacher and principal in Tioga, North Dakota. I had stopped in to visit and attend a basketball game with them. A teacher of dramatics, music, and English, who was also a soloist at community activities and even the Farmers Union meetings, was sitting between my sister and brother-in-law. I sat down next to my sister. It was the first and last time my sister sat between the two of us. Florence and I had casually met before, but this night I walked her home, and we fell madly in love with each other.

God's miraculous yes answer to my prayers

We were married in Tioga, which was Florence's hometown, a little over one year later. We had a beautiful summer wedding with a reception at Florence's parents' home. We even had a movie of our wedding, which we took after the ceremony. Our honeymoon was our trip to the state of Washington. On our way to Pasco, we decided to go a little out of our way and visit the Seattle area. My mother had packed fresh chicken for us to take along, and we had fifteen dozen eggs in the car with us, so it was easy to fix breakfast each morning for ourselves. We didn't think about using a cooler!

Florence is the reason that our churches had good and well-attended children's choirs, a red-vested boys' choir, and six choirs at Trinity Lutheran in Hawthorne, California. Singing praises to the Lord at services every Sunday of the year were 178 choral members. Florence was constantly at my side to help me understand and appreciate music. She shared the gift that God had given her and was always available for solos and other musical work. Even though the Lord didn't work a miracle to perfect my voice, He gave me more than that through Florence and her musical skills.

At this writing, we have been "making music together" for sixty-nine years! "Praise God from whom all blessings flow! Praise Him all creatures here below, Praise Him above ye heavenly hosts, Praise Father, Son, and Holy Ghost!"

CHAPTER 2

PASCO, WASHINGTON—
THE HANFORD PROJECT

INTO MISSION-DRIVEN INSECURITIES

This section title is not in reference to an investment into stocks, patents, or any fly-by-night scheme. The insecurities that I am alluding to started with my facing the ministry, especially during the time of my searching the Lord's will for my life's work. It started at Bible camp when I was only sixteen years old. This consideration continued uppermost in my mind through the next two Bible camps, which brought me to the summer after I finished high school. It was at this time the Lord laid it upon my heart to renew and to make a full commitment to Jesus Christ. As I look back, I realize it was an augmentation or a further step of the commitment of confirmation about three years before. We had the most stirring speakers at these camps. Their messages dwelt on spiritual growth of Christians but with an overwhelming emphasis on full commitment to Jesus Christ and to the future. I had heard it in my own parish from my own pastor; however, in the Bible camp setting with two hundred to three hundred youth my age, it made a greater impression. One speaker was Andrew Burgess, who was a missionary in

China. He later became a professor at Luther Theological Seminary in St. Paul, from which I graduated. Andrew Burgess was such an exciting speaker and extremely motivational. He was friendly and congenial and loved life. He was also out there with all of the boys and girls and faculty members playing ball. I remember him yelling out to the pitcher of the pastor's team, "We are all behind you!" and everyone, from the first basemen to the right fielder, stood physically behind the pitcher.

Andrew Burgess brought to our attention the great need in China, the excitement of seeing souls saved, and the primitiveness of the Lutheran Church in that country. He told us about the unusual dangers Burt and Daniel Nelson experienced in China facing the Communists, who were at that time only a threat and not in power. He told us how Burt Nelson had been killed by the Communist terrorists (they didn't call them terrorists at that time). The Lord lay upon my heart to start praying about going into the ministry so that I could be prepared to go to China. I pictured the Chinese as uncivilized, unsophisticated, and uneducated. I was wrong on all three. However, I felt that an ungifted farm boy from North Dakota might be able to serve the Lord in an area like that, even though I knew I would have no chance in America.

My second year in college was a time of decision. What was I going to do with my life; what did the Lord want for me? China came back into my mind; however, six or seven more years in college and seminary were ahead of me, and I was struggling to make ends meet financially. Most importantly, my parents needed me on the farm. The vague pull of the farm or an easy life of financial security didn't begin to compare with the compelling power of the Holy Spirit directing me into full-time mission work.

With the help of Harold Brown, my mentor through many years and also the man who solicited students at Bible camp and strongly influenced me to go to college, my coursework, including Greek, was selected. At that time it was common knowledge that if you were going on to seminary or if you were going into the ministry, you had to start taking Greek your sophomore year in college.

Let me skip over to my main theme of this chapter: mission-driven insecurity. It was my last year at the seminary, and we had already been put on a fast schedule because of the war. Between my second and last year, we were exempt from internship, which would ordinarily be one year. I already had taught Bible school three summers, and one of these summers, I worked as an assistant pastor with Norris Stoa in Parshall, North Dakota, so I wouldn't be losing out on much. I found myself graduating from seminary in January rather than a year and a half later in June. I was only twenty-four years of age and single and had just become interested in a beautiful young lady from Tioga, North Dakota, but I didn't know where that might go.

In October and November of 1944, we were to determine our location in the ministry. Most of us would receive invitations from call committees, from individuals, and from different missions. I deliberated on whether I should go into the military chaplaincy; however, it appeared that there was not a need at this late a date in the progress of the war. My early motivation to go into the ministry was China, so during that fall, I met with the foreign missions committee of our Lutheran Church and told them that I was ready to go. The year before, some of my classmates were called to China, and they were studying Chinese in Berkeley, California. If the mission-board plan would continue, anyone from our class who was going to Chinese missions would do the same. At that time, China was being threatened with a takeover by powerful Communists.

After weeks, the foreign-mission board determined that this was not the time to send missionaries there, inasmuch as some had already been imprisoned for as long as three years. This group included Judy Scogerboe and several others. The mission-board determination was "not now."

I had indicated to my teachers and inquirers, including district presidents, that I was interested in West Coast emergency missions if I could not go to China. Dr. Foss, the district president of our Pacific Northwest District, came to talk to me about an unusual development in the Pasco, Richland, and Kennewick, Washington, area. The Lutheran Church had very little exposure there. Three struggling little congregations had been ministering there for a few years under the direction of one pastor, and now they were calling for a separate pastor for each of the three churches.

Something unusual had happened in that area to motivate one of the most fantastic growths of any place in the United States at that time. No one knew what they were doing out there at Richland, but everyone knew it had something to do with defense and maybe an abrupt ending of the war. I chose to accept the call from Home Missions to Pasco, Washington. I was so naïve and so committed to serving Jesus Christ that I didn't pay any attention to the financial insecurities of my vocation. I was also naïve about what was being built at Richland. I'd vaguely heard that my one classmate and good friend was going to West Fargo with a salary of $2,400 a year. That was a third larger than my salary, but it wasn't until we got out to Pasco that I realized it would be very difficult to live on my actual salary—$1,800 a year. At that time in the ministry of our church, no one to my knowledge even considered the wife working an outside job. She was to be her husband's helpmate in the truest sense. If anyone ever thought of it, it was "far out."

With the help of my parents, I did buy a car before I left the seminary. At that time in '45, the newest car was a 1940 or '41. No cars were manufactured for civilians during that period. I bought a well-used Chevrolet with four old tires for $800 in St. Paul. The tires on this car were a story in themselves. At that time, it was very difficult to buy tires, unless you bought ones that had been collected three or four years earlier and had been piled in a big heap and now were not needed for military purposes. Therefore, they were now available and supposedly very reliable, but it wasn't at all uncommon to have a flat tire on any of my trips.

After graduation on January 25 and ordination on February 25, and having been engaged to my life partner the night before my ordination, I was ready to go out to my first parish with mission-driven insecurity in an old car, alone, and going for the first time west of the Rocky Mountains. To a prairie farm boy, the West Coast seemed as far away as China. It was rather comforting to my parents, even though they never doubted that this was God's will, that Henry Johnson rode with me to Spokane, Washington. He had been a good friend of our family for years and would help pay for the gas. At that time, we were still on gas rationing, even though you could get a few more A stamps for going to your permanent job. The A stamps were given to people who didn't have any priorities. An A stamp would qualify you to buy two gallons of gas a week. A man who owned a large Packard car wondered why they would give him only two gallons a week. A friend of his came up with the answer: in case of fire, you could back your car out of the garage. It was not uncommon to utilize farm-rationed gasoline for necessary trips. My first night in Washington was at a service center. I knew the pastor and his wife who directed this. They increased my feelings of insecurity when they told me that the area where I was going had some unusual purposes in the defense and in the winning of the war. There were people living there from all over the United States from various backgrounds, and a lot of people there who needed a pastor.

This further convinced me that it was God's will that I should go there rather than the chaplaincy at this late date and not China at this time. On my way to Washington, I stopped in Missoula, Montana, to visit my former high-school English teacher and her husband. This happened to be Florence's cousin, who had been in China. Yes, Marian Borstad Daehlin was a great attraction because her maiden name was the same name as my precious sweetheart who I anticipated marrying in six months. One of the other reasons for stopping was because I hadn't gotten China out of my mind yet. It was lingering, at least. They also suggested that my decision to go to Pasco was a good one at this time.

Arrival in Pasco
As I arrived in Pasco, I was not greeted by any bands or choirs or even individuals. I finally found the place where I would be staying temporarily

in a basement room. This room was comfortable and served OK as the parsonage for six weeks until I was able to improve my conditions by renting a room in the basement of the Congregational pastor's home only a block from my church. I had many conversations during this time with my fiancé, trying to convince her to have our wedding that summer rather than postpone it a year or so. I at least convinced her that we should set the date, and she in turn convinced me that we should extend it to the very end of the summer: August 22. Whew, one of my most important insecurities had now been affirmed. A life decision of great importance!

Letter of Love

May, 1945
11:30 p.m. Wed.　　　　　　　　　*"Serve Him with gladness"*
My Dearest,

Just came back from my last Adult Instruction class. This has been about the busiest day I've ever spent here, one thing after another. Today is bulletin day—guess I work rather slowly but it takes 3 hours just to prepare it and make a dummy copy. A young fellow stopped in and wants his wedding next Sunday eve.—so we talked it over for some time. I suppose you know what I am doing? I'm building up a case to show you how badly I need your help, your ambition and your love. Ah, it's going to be wonderful to have one that cares right near me and one who I think the world of with me. I need an organist for there are four weddings that are coming up too. Don't take it wrong dear, you know those things are secondary and you first but it will be great to do things together too…won't it?

Thanks for the 99.9% of your love. When do I get the other 10th?

The more I am around here and meet young wives and girls the more thankful I am for you. I really feel sorry for some of the husbands…then I wonder how come I'm so fortunate to rate F.L.B. I am plenty happy and thankful to you and for you Sweetheart!

Tomorrow you go into another day of school. How many pupils do you have now? Isn't it different to prepare when you don't know how many there will be? I have had to prepare for 10–30 sometimes.

Must say good night as tomorrow we have Ladies Aid, Luther League Committee meeting, two or three important letters I need to write, and a visit with some of the ladies for arranging further for Bible school and then more sermon preparation. It's all fun though and always something different. It will be much better though when my Darling will be here. I love you Florence…So Very Much.

Love,
Orv

It was so exciting to think of August 22, only four months away.

The Hanford project

The danger and insecurity of the area was unknown to everyone except a handful of people, and a very interesting thing developed the last week I was at the seminary. Our very austere, formal, and revered president had a reception for all of the seminary graduates now going into their work throughout the world. When he asked me where I was going, he told me that his son-in-law, Milton Grimsrud, and his daughter, Milton's wife, Solveig, had started a ministry in Richland under the National Lutheran Council, which was sort of a combination of all the synods. The government permitted one Protestant church, one Catholic, one Jewish synagogue, and a Lutheran church in the area. They mentioned how the Richland area had been designated by the government as an out-of-bounds area for almost everything except the workers for two or three years because they were building the most secretive weapons for the war. They did mention that out in the Hanford area, a district on the other side of Richland, they had built a number of factories after moving out all of the farmers and anybody that lived in that area. It was a five-mile distance between each of the five factories. While this was being built, there were thousands living in temporary towns, dormitories, and barracks around the area. Richland was the maintenance city of whatever they were building there with a population of thirty thousand. It had grown from its original size of fewer than one thousand people.

Each contact that I made previous to reaching Pasco, Washington, in the south central district of the state caused a greater interest for me. I realized that God had truly called me and that there was a tremendous need. Pasco, only five miles from Richland, had grown from a little cow town of two to three thousand to about thirty thousand. People moved in and out quite rapidly, and there was a large, temporary home development for the many navy people. We called them "the navy homes." It was common to hear navy airplanes take off from the Pasco airport, one every minute, for their training exercises. I was able to go out into the area of construction with a special pass and with Pastor Grimsrud. This factory continued to be built with additional programs even before and during the Korean War. They would have piles of lumber that would be blocks long, maybe twenty feet wide, and equally as high.

I went back home in August for our wedding. I planned to go two weeks before the wedding to help Dad with the harvest. I had become a very accomplished combine operator. Maybe my father gave me this evaluation mistakenly or intentionally to motivate me to come home by running the combine for two or three weeks during my vacations for the first twelve years in the ministry. I received enough money from Dad's generosity to pay for the car that I had just bought. It was a real godsend. The Depression was over, and the crops were coming back.

The secret is out
A few days before our wedding, I went down to the mailbox a little less than a quarter mile from the house to pick up the mail. I opened the *Williston Herald* and the headline was "Atomic Bomb Dropped on Hiroshima." Beneath that it said that this bomb was made in New Mexico and Richland, Washington. Now I knew the big secret!

Hanford was a 586-square-mile site created in 1943 as part of the Manhattan Project (America's effort to develop the atomic bomb, the most destructive instrument to be known on earth). I remember well taking a Sunday afternoon drive to this gated area. High fences with signs greeted us, announcing that no one was allowed to enter this area. Forbidden! No entrance! Only six months after my arrival, the first bomb was dropped, and now we all knew.

The puzzle and the great unknown concerning what was happening at Richland, Washington, that caused all the great influx of people to the tri-city area was now solved. Richland was a fine city, and many of the people were sent in to clean up the atomic waste that was stored in 100-by-100-square-foot cement vats buried under the ground. We were told that these would never leak. Never say never! They did start leaking after many years, and the site was contaminated with hazardous substances, including both radionuclides and chemical waste. Every so often our three daughters, who were all born in Pasco, receive an invitation to share if they have had any related illness due to the radiation. Billions of gallons of contaminated water were discharged into the soil, and the cows ate the grass, so in turn the milk could have been polluted by atomic waste.

As far as I know, there have been no physical effects on the people I know. Sometimes we believe that the cancer epidemic is a little greater there than in other places though.

The dangers of a factory only a few miles from us was made very clear when we found out about the devastating destruction of the atomic bomb in Japan. It appears that the government had carefully built parts in different areas so that the danger would be less in each place. It had been a well-kept secret, and it was the most significant thing in concluding the war with Japan without having to sacrifice thousands of our young men in an invasion of Japan, like we had to do in Europe. The European war had ended, and Germany had surrendered some months before. I discovered the insecurities of America when, even though we'd won the war in Europe and were close to winning the war in Japan, we lost our president. This loss increased our insecurity, as our president had been in for three terms, and many of our youth had only known Roosevelt in their lifetimes. However, Harry Truman in many ways fulfilled the classic statement that is credited to him, "The buck stops here."

Securities and uncertainties continue
At that time I was challenged with building a place for eighty people to worship as well as a parish education basement that would hold thirty to forty children. This small beginning increased rapidly as we grew in seven years to a church of three hundred members with a large number in Sunday school. The insecurity changed when we built and made room for almost three times as many people in church and in Sunday school.

Where you come from does not determine where God can take you
Paul addresses the young Titus, saying, "He must hold firmly to the trustworthy message as it has been taught, so that he can encourage others by sound doctrine and refute those who oppose it" (Titus 1:9).

Titus also includes some wonderful reminders of God's love and kindness toward us, which brought Him to send His Son to save us, "not because of our righteous things we had done but because of His mercy. We have been saved by grace through Jesus Christ, thereby having the sure hope of eternal life" (Titus 3:5).

A mission-driven ministry
My first task in this small, very ingrown, and shortsighted congregation was to find the support we needed to sustain ourselves. The financial insecurity of the church changed when the stewardship and the availability of money changed. In my naïveté and idealism, I prohibited any sales for the purpose of making money as related to the church, stating that all the money for the church had to be raised by giving. In addition

to that, we inaugurated a pledge system, an envelope system, and a stewardship drive a whole month in the fall of the year. At first, this small group of people wondered how the Home Mission Board could have made such a mistake in calling in an inexperienced and idealistic young pastor such as me.

But the Lord was merciful and gracious to me, the parishioners, and the church. He sent us many new members—generous new people—and there was an overall acceptance of the new Bible-based giving program. One person, the chairman of the trustees and the man who had built most of the furniture, especially the beautifully built and polished pews, never accepted the aggressive ministry. He had been the key man in that church, and the early meetings started in his house. His two daughters and sons-in-law also were members and also resisted the new campaign.

As the church grew, we were no longer in need of the rental money from the family that rented the basement apartment in our parsonage. We wanted to make over the basement of the parsonage across the street from church into a parish education unit. By this time, this one man was the only objector to the advancing power throughout the congregation. As they were digging an outside entrance into our parsonage basement, this man stood in the very hole that was being made for the entrance, and one of the young men jokingly but sternly said, "Get out of there, or we'll cover you up." I was not there, or I would have been terribly hurt and would have been full of apologies. Years later, this man adjusted to the missionary work of the church, including changing the basement from a moneymaker to a Sunday school–maker.

I should inject here that his family all came back to the church, but he did not, during the time I was there. However, my last call before I left was with him, for by then we had become good friends. He acknowledged in his more generous moments that the buying of the parsonage a year after we had arrived and changing the basement into a Sunday school building was a very good thing.

Guests always welcome

It appears to me that I was so naïve and so eager to save souls that I did at times endanger my family, and especially my wife, by accommodating homeless people who at the time we called bums. We were in a railroad center, and people were still riding these freight trains, as we were near the atomic factory and the work there attracted many of the less stable transient people. Our houseguests from out of town would be astonished when we told them that we had a man who slept on our porch who had come begging for food. Florence was always prepared with sandwiches in the refrigerator ready to give to someone in need. Later on, they would sleep in the church and eat with us. We had an open-door policy, since we were so close to the church. We would not only welcome people on Sunday to church, but we would also welcome them to dinner after church or to our house during the week.

Flood and plane crash

I had started a church in Grandview, Washington, north of Pasco, about two years after I arrived. I would go visiting door to door one day a week and make contact with any others who had shown an interest in the church. I would have a worship service every Sunday evening. One of the families from First Lutheran in Pasco had moved to this area and helped with the beginnings of this congregation. Also, a ladies aid society, which had been meeting previously but had no connection to a church body as yet, helped. This motivated me to organize Emmanuel Lutheran Church in Grandview in 1948. Pastor Grimsrud would assist me whenever available and when needed.

Early in the year as the ice pack melted off of the Columbia River, we had the greatest flood ever seen before or since near Pasco. There was no way we could drive in any direction, especially up to Grandview. An entrepreneur had reactivated some old two-man war planes to be used for emergencies in our area.

I hired him to fly me for an important meeting that I had in the church. As we were landing at the small airport on Grandview's gravel runway, thumping, clicking weird noises were coming from the engine. I felt something was wrong. Before I knew it, we were spinning around on the ground without any landing gear extended. After some loud bangs and smashing, screeching sounds, we stopped spinning around, resting not on the wheels of the plane but on the body. There was silence. We didn't say a word. We were in shock. The plane was wrecked, but were we OK? Our limbs seemed intact, so we began making our way through the wreck of the plane. We finally got out, thanking the Lord for no fire, no bruises, and no broken bones from this.

Extraordinary experience! I went on and didn't miss my meeting.

Whenever I would drive by that small airport in Grandview, Washington, and look behind the main building, I could see the old, wrecked World War II plane sitting next to the garbage heap of old airplane parts. I would stop and say a prayer of thanks to God for saving me.

HE SHOT A POLICEMAN

What a heartbreaking time for a family! I was in shock. I opened the newspaper on a quiet Monday morning to the glaring headline on the front page announcing "Policeman Shot!" The article reported that a thief, while trying to steal some guns in a town some distance away, had been apprehended. Unfortunately, in the commotion a gunfight had broken out, and this man had shot one of the policemen. I was shocked when I saw the shooter's name because I had met him and knew his wife and extended family. He had attended our church once some time ago. I was saddened to read this story about this thief-murderer whom I had known and to learn of the tragic turn his life had taken.

In orange jail suit

What could I do? I immediately went to where he was imprisoned, which was about one hundred miles away. It was one of the saddest days in my ministry to see this man behind bars. The last time I had seen him he was clean shaven and nicely dressed in a light summer suit, now he was in an orange jail uniform, unkempt, and a mess. I remember one thing he said to me, which sticks in my mind: "No matter what happens to me, will you help to make sure my wonderful son is reared as a good Christian man?" At this time his son was four years old, very alert, and so cute. His wife, the mother of the boy, was a fine person whose mother and dad I knew quite well.

Later that year, this man escaped from jail and remained free for many months. However, as almost always happens, he did get caught again, and this life of crime landed him back in prison. I went twice to visit him there while he was in solitary confinement. He could have no outside visitors. He had no mail or newspapers, and instead of three meals a day, he had two. I could get a message to him only through a designated guard. After each visit with him, I left feeling very downhearted and distressed by his situation.

He did try to escape at least one more time and then finally learned his lesson. I understand through some acquaintances that he finally had become somewhat of a model prisoner. After another forty years of the prison life, he did get out, but it was to an entirely different world, different friends, and few remaining family members. No one is sure if he got out due to old age, good behavior, or for medical reasons.

Only the Lord knows why a man like this would do the things he did at such a great cost. The wickedness of humankind is what caused the Lord to go to the cross and shed His blood for our sins. I had prayed and hoped that he had a change of heart before he met his Maker many years ago. His son and his wife, who had divorced him and remarried, remained loyal Christians through the years.

NOT A CENT FOR LODGING

Traveling coast to coast
Who arranged that our relatives and a friend would live a day apart across the United States? This was a perfect travel setup for our family of four.

Seriously, it was strange to realize that the people we wanted to visit on our trip to New York lived about a day apart. This had all been organized ahead of time and could have worked well, except that we had not planned where we would stay in New York. In the back of my mind, I expected to find a dorm room that would be suitable for our family.

A house found

A phone call to Florence's cousin Marian Borstad Daehlin and Rader, her husband, proved that God was in the mix of our adventure. Rader Daehlin was the pastor of the large Trinity Lutheran in Brooklyn, New York. Marian was not only Florence's cousin but had also been my English teacher my freshman year at Epping High School.

As I visited with Rader on the phone, I told him the reason for our visit to New York. He asked, "Where are you staying?" I replied, "We don't know as yet." He then said, "Come and stay here for the next three weeks, as I am leaving soon. Marian is already at our Minnesota cabin to avoid the terrible, humid heat of New York in July. I will be joining her in a few of days. You can take care of our house and small yard. It's easy to take the subway into the city, and it only costs twenty-five cents."

Oh thank you, Lord, I said to myself. How great for Florence and the girls to be in a nice home rather than stuck in a dorm room in the city. Since we would be staying at this house as guests, we were very happy to save the money for lodging. The $700 that had been set aside for the three-plus weeks we needed to stay was almost depleted to pay for attending summer school at the Biblical Theological Seminary in Manhattan.

For a prairie farm boy to hop onto a New York subway each day alone was scary, figuring out routes and where to get on and off, plus the pushing and shoving to get to a connecting train to Manhattan made it even scarier. I figured it out, and the time at seminary was a time of great learning. I experienced a renewal for my ministry some seven years after completing Luther Seminary in St. Paul.

Florence, Ilene, and Dorene spent the days in this comfortable home where the girls made friends in the neighborhood and even had a lemonade stand out in front of the house. They also enjoyed catching lightning bugs in the evenings. The country farm girl, Florence, together with Dorene and Ilene, bravely took the subway into New York to meet me in the afternoons. Then we would sightsee and experience the city that we knew only from books. Florence wasn't sure why she would get stared at by people on the subway, who would eye her first and then look at the girls. Perhaps most people had not seen such blond and blue-eyed children before in this East Coast city. The Statue of Liberty, museums, Central Park, and our first-ever pro baseball game at Yankee Stadium were just a few of our adventures. We spent our weekends seeing historical sites along the eastern shore from Boston to Washington, DC.

Our trip back to Washington State was filled with stops to visit friends and family. We renewed friendships with my mentor, Pastor Norris Stoa, and his family and my aunt and uncle in Pawnee, Illinois, as well as cousins in West Union, Iowa, which made our coast-to-coast trip pleasurable and created many lasting memories.

READY TO SHOOT HIS WIFE AND ANOTHER MAN

In my first parish in Pasco, Washington, our church office was located off the front porch, in a front bedroom in our parsonage. Our home was just across the street from the church. Because our town was a great railroad town with two main railroads crossing in our little city, we had men frequently stopping for a handout or in need of a place to sleep. The church and our back porch became places to sleep.

I came home one evening a little early, and as I walked into the front room, my wife, Florence, told me that a man at the door wanted to talk with me. I invited him immediately into my office, as he seemed to be a perturbed person, hardly saying hello. After I went around to my side of the desk, he pulled out two revolvers and held them in his hands and then laid them both on the desk in front of me, saying, "Can God forgive me if I shoot my wife and another man?" Can you guess how I felt? Relieved, of course, but very concerned about his well-being.

He continued to talk in a random fashion and said both guns were fully loaded and had been ready to fire at any moment for the past two days as he met every train that came into town. If his wife and her "friend" had stepped off any one of those trains, he would have shot both of them. Eventually, he did calm down, talked somewhat rationally, and changed his mind about committing murder.

After he left that night, I did not observe the privilege of privacy that I could have invoked as a pastor. I called the police to search him out.

Two or three days later, I stopped over at the address he had given me because he had not called me as I had asked. I knocked, and a very confident and outgoing young lady came to the door. I named the man I was looking for and asked if he lived there. She responded, "Oh, my husband left just this morning for Alaska."

I am sorry that I can't claim any exciting story about him becoming converted, or as to whether I had helped him, but a few years later, when I returned for a church anniversary, the wife had become a member of the church and had settled down. She had remarried, and they were in church both times I had returned. I guess I'll never know what happened to him.

SEEING MY FIRST TELEVISION SET

A trip to a church convention

Florence and I had anticipated and planned for a year for the possibility of attending a national all-Lutheran church convention in San Francisco. Dorene was three years old, and we thought we could do this as a family. It was a long drive from Pasco, Washington, and gasoline was twenty cents a gallon, but we made it possible by sharing the costs with three passengers—Pastor Milton Grimsrud, Mrs. Marner, and her daughter.

Off we traveled in our old car, which we'd bought as a five-year-old model, as no cars were manufactured between 1941 and 1946 when all efforts were directed toward winning the war. The prewar Chevy made the trip in good shape with the four adults and two children. We stayed overnight with friends in Bend, Oregon, saving a night's lodging, but otherwise hardly ever stopped on our way to San Francisco. Following the convention and experiencing some shopping, I saw my first television set in a storefront window at age twenty-eight. I wondered how the guy got in the box, and could he see me? How could these pictures and sounds from across the nation show up in that box where I could see it? I was really in awe! In San Francisco, we also visited Fisherman's Wharf, Golden Gate Park, and some of the other San Francisco attractions. Florence, Dorene, and I went on and drove the old car to Southern California. The sights of Hollywood, Hollywood Bowl, Long Beach, and the ocean were all things we had read about and now were experiencing firsthand. We stayed with my parents' dear friends in Redlands, California, Mr. and Mrs. Ed Retzlaff, where fresh oranges from the groves surrounding their home were in abundance.

As we were already so far south, we decided to spend one more day and go to another country—Mexico. We posed for a family picture, donkey and all, on the streets of Tijuana, and it is a keepsake to this day. To save money on two nights' lodging, as well as visit further with dear childhood friends, we returned to the Retzlaffs after our day trip to Mexico. We left very early the following morning to get back to our home in two days, stopping for one short night of rest in our almost sixteen-hundred-mile trip back to Washington.

A NICE, GODLY MAN CHANGED

His actions had become so erratic. He was sad and just a different person. Our friend had been in a terrible accident and was left a changed and angry man. Luckily, no crimes were committed, but he had a gun that he should not have had because he was a sick man. We had done some work together at church, and one evening, many days after the accident, apparently he was overcome and lost it. His actions were bizarre and dangerous. He was admitted into a mental hospital for months at a time, hoping for rehabilitation. He would come home for a period of time but never could stay and never again was the same man as before the accident.

Some scary things happened in connection with the church, at our home, and even around Florence. No one was ever hurt or harmed in any way, but we had to be on the alert. In this day and age, we would call it "stalking." When he would have a breakdown, he was like a loose cannon and would end up at the mental hospital some 150 miles from his home.

We would go to visit him frequently. Often I would take his wife and mother along, and we would have a picnic on the hospital grounds. Dorene remembers this, as many times Florence and the girls would come along. After a visit, we would stop at a park to play games and have some fun on our trip. When this man came out for picnics, he seemed almost normal and back to his old self. There was no danger then, and the nurses were near if we needed help. Later on we learned that they had given him a lobotomy, which made him docile and mild mannered. Today lobotomies are rarely performed.

The rest of his life he lived in the hospital under treatment and under the care of doctors and nurses. He never did return to his loving family, wife, and two children. His wife and parents were pillars in the church and truly wonderful people.

The Lord knew his heart before this tragic accident. This man was not personally responsible for not being in his right mind. We don't understand why these things happen, but we know God knows everything better than we do, and His love is so great in these situations even though we may question and wonder.

CHAPTER 3

SACRAMENTO, CALIFORNIA—CAPITAL CITY

THE HOLY SPIRIT MAKES A CHURCH GROW

At a South Sacramento development of new houses, parents and children filled the recently paved streets and empty fields where vegetables once grew, waiting for the earth movers to come and clear off the land to build more new houses. More building in that area promised a new community for fast-growing Sacramento, capital of California. My loyal, talented wife, our three daughters, and I gave up our very successful, joyful congregation, new church building, friends, and home of seven years to answer God's call. Just as Abraham left the land of Mesopotamia for a new land, we traveled to a new state and a new community where we knew no one and had no home. We did this to respond to His call to reach souls for Christ so that heaven will be their promised home when it is time for them to leave this earth.

Transition

Traveling one thousand miles from Pasco, Washington, to Sacramento was a time of processing the coming changes. It began to sink in that this would become our new home. Even without friends to welcome us and no one to offer my Norwegian wife a cup of coffee or a place to sleep, we still thought we had come to a land "flowing with milk and honey." We were able to find an inexpensive motel with one room available in which to stay. Unknown to us, the plumbing didn't work, and that lasted for the first few weeks. Nonetheless, we didn't have to walk too far to use substitute facilities, at least not as far as at my North Dakota home, which had four bedrooms and a path.

I had one day to unload our car and get settled in the motel room because I needed to begin calling door to door to let people know about the new church being organized. Florence spent the day alone, caring for the children and assuring the girls—and perhaps herself—that they would soon have new friends and a new church.

As a family we would go to the wonderful hundred-acre Capitol Park for relaxing and some alone time. You can imagine how much that meant to six-week-old Nelene, three-year-old Ilene, and Dorene, a six-year-old first grader. The girls would run around, and we'd have family games and a time just for us. Florence and I loved this.

Aren't we going home?
Ilene really touched her mother's heart and even caused a few tears to flow when she would often say, "We are going back to our home in Pasco, aren't we, Mommy? Aren't we, Mommy…please? Aren't we?" It got both of us when she said, "I left my little shovel and pail in my sandbox in Pasco, and we can go back so I can play in my sandbox, can't we, Mommy? Can't we, Daddy?" Of course in my heart I was missing our first home, dear friends, and the familiar, but we knew there was a plan for us in the Fruitridge area of Sacramento.

Public school—a shocking change
Dorene found the first days of school most disconcerting—no prayers, no chapel, and no singing of familiar songs. As she got acquainted with the public schools, there were many acceptable substitutes. She did get

into trouble once when the teacher sent her out to get a stubborn student to come in from recess. The child enjoyed the playground much more than the classroom. Well, Dorene simply followed orders by dragging the small child off the playground by one arm into the classroom. Dorene was familiar with strict orders and discipline from her private school, so she interpreted it to mean "You come in by yourself, or I'll make you because the teacher said so."

Starting from nothing
Ten days after our arrival, a parish visitor came to help me, sent out from the church headquarters in Minneapolis. Ione was a good-looking, attractively dressed thirty-six-year-old woman who began the door-to-door canvassing, inviting people to a new congregation. Many thought she was the Avon lady and welcomed her and the conversation. Ione became our church secretary, piano teacher, and choir director under the title of Parish Worker. As an aside, she was a daughter of one of the Bush brothers who had been an early leader of the 3M Corporation in Minnesota. We did find her a motel room where the plumbing worked. Florence also discovered that her parents and Ione's were from the same area in Minnesota and they had walked to school together as children. What a small world!

A dead place became full of life
In addition to getting acquainted with the area and calling door to door at least four hours a day, we were busy trying to find a meeting place for worship. We met up with a very congenial John Bowers at South Sacramento Lawn Cemetery. This was located near the area of the new housing development where we were looking to build the church. He said that on Sunday mornings the chapel in the mausoleum was available for services. This was also the area used for funeral services, so you can imagine on Decoration Day and other special holidays how the walls and halls were filled with flowers and on patriotic holidays with flags of red, white, and blue.

Flyers were designed and printed as handouts with the starting date of our new church. Palm Sunday, a week before Easter, was a desirable time to begin services because many people were more inclined to attend church on Easter than at other times. The church was filled with young and old in just four weeks.

A four-year-old congregation and staff ready to build again

The congregation, which was initially sponsored by the denomination, no longer needed any operational help eight months after starting from scratch in a new area of Sacramento. They weren't only self-supporting after eight months but also gave up their home-mission status, thus making the subsidy available to another new starting church.

The paid staff of three elementary teachers, a full-time office secretary, and a pastor as well as an assistant pastor saw this new six-room school building plus ten offices built in less than twelve months by eighty-five volunteer laborers. They saw the school grow into a kindergarten through eighth grade in six years. The school eventually reached four hundred students.

The church grew to twelve hundred souls over seven years, and I served as principal of the elementary school for its first six years. The lead carpenter and I served as the co-contractors for the two building programs in the first five to six years.

The Sunday school was very effective in getting all the neighborhood children off the streets on Sunday morning to the extent that seven hundred enrolled and attended the Sunday school all twelve months of the year.

Christian day school and church

Ilene and Dorene attended Gloria Dei School, with grades kindergarten through third. Each year we would add a grade and, of course, more students. We had wonderful teachers from the Midwest who came and were excellent in helping to get the school started. Small class sizes and having religion every day were real drawing cards for young parents looking for the best schools for their children. They, in turn, became interested in being involved in the church community. I remember the school-naming contest, which the two Petersen brothers won by naming the school Gloria Dei. The Petersen families have been members and leaders of the church through the years.

A large school building with eight classrooms was added six years after the beginning. By that time, we had grades kindergarten through eighth. The church building became a parish hall in later years, and four years after I left, a new, beautiful church was built because of the growth of this congregation. Four hundred students attended this very well respected educational facility in the '90s and early 2000s.

What a plan God had for us, and this was only the beginning! These seven unbelievable years of ministry at Fruitridge Lutheran, later known as Gloria Dei Lutheran, played a most significant role in my ministry as well as for our family.

One Person Everyone Says Is Beyond Extraordinary

Florence milked her favorite cows even on her wedding day. She stood as the most adorably dressed bride in front of the altar at her most precious church, which was packed with friends and family, and gave up her wonderful life in that small town. It was Wednesday night, August 22, 1945, at 8:00 p.m., in the Tioga farming community of North Dakota. She was a farmer's daughter, high-school teacher, and homebound daughter before I married her.

She gave it all up for someone who took her a thousand miles away to the unknown, wild, and wooly West, to Pasco, Washington. She became the queen to one of the luckiest prairie farm boys and unknown pastors in the world—me!

She redeemed herself a little by becoming one of the most admired vocal soloists in her church and new city. Many knew of her talents in college, as she was a soloist in the Augsburg College Choir in Minneapolis. She became the director of her own large children's choir, confirmation choir, and red-vested boys' choir in each of the churches that I pastored. She had a keen sense of how to make each individual child feel important, and even if the child started out as monotone, she could develop some sense of melodic utterances within him or her.

As a result of her training, the children became good, strong singers. Her musical abilities became well known when she organized children's choirs from other churches along with ours and held festivals for all churches and their choirs, who participated in the thrill of singing in children's mass choir festivals. She would organize each choir to contribute one song and perform it and then import another director, who would direct the grand finale song with all of the choirs participating at once, an experience many children would never forget. At the same time, she continued to direct the many choirs at our weekly church services. During our evening services, she was most happy to have one of her choirs participate, and it was a wonderful way of making evening services more attractive.

She was the vocal soloist of choice

In addition to all the above areas of ministry, she soon became the vocal soloist of choice at most of our weddings. It wasn't surprising that, at least during the month of June, we would have up to three weddings each Saturday. All of this became just one of the exciting opportunities of service for her.

You can see why everyone loved and adored her.

It isn't unusual to this day for people to call me and share that Florence sang at their wedding or even at a friend's funeral, whether it was sixty years ago or sixteen.

Somehow, some way, she managed all of this without ever neglecting her children or her husband. She involved all of us in that part of her life. The children and high-school youth of our family didn't only have a great music teacher, but they also took pride in the fact that their mom was the director. I'd love to have her sing at my funeral someday.

Musical recital with 111 pianos

First Piano Festival
SACRAMENTO MEMORIAL AUDITORIUM
Sunday, June 7, 1959

Our oldest daughter, Dorene, experienced an unforgettable event at the piano festival in Sacramento, California, in which mother and daughter played a duet on one piano along with two hundred other participants on 111 pianos in the Sacramento Memorial Auditorium. For all practical purposes, it was Dorene's annual piano recital, as her teacher, Edna Stanbridge Smith, who planned and created great enthusiasm for piano lessons, was one of the organizers of this massive piano festival involving eight hundred participants. The participants were divided into six groups. Dorene was in group four, and the mother-daughter duo was in group six. I also just found out from our friend Joyce Karlstad Borrud that she was in group three. Piano students never get the experience of playing with many participants as band and orchestra students do. It was memorable.

A piano company in Sacramento loaned the organization the 111 pianos used for the event, and the conductor was the director of the Sacramento Philharmonic Orchestra. It was unforgettable for both the performers and the audience and especially for our mother-daughter combo.

Music experiences

The stories, experiences, and funny events remind me of the fun we had at the choir parties, such as watermelon busts, marshmallow roasts, and ice cream or ice-cream bar treats that Florence organized. This kept kids motivated to sing and to have fun doing it while gathering with their church friends. Talk about having fun—Peggy, Dorene's friend, mentioned that she was in awe because Dorene had a mom who yodeled! Great fun.

Florence would often sing on our weekly radio program, *Moments of Refreshment*. (I don't think she yodeled there.) I still use some of those solos on tape at occasions and services when she is unable to attend. Her red-vested boys' choir remembered the trips that they made from LA to First Lutheran in Vista, California, as a never-to-be-forgotten experience. I know of no one who could be a more willing or more sensitive and loving mother, wife, grandmother, and now great-grandmother to six little ones as Florence.

I praise God for her, her parents, her home, and her church, as they influenced her to be the perfect wife, mother, and teacher whom we all love so much.

There was something she didn't like

I would like to share with you a very human part of her, in that I once got her a gift for which she was not very thankful. On each day that it was supposed to be used, she would pray that it would rain, and it did for most of the ten golf lessons that I had scheduled as a gift for her.

The result? Well, she was kind enough to play every once in a while just to make me feel good. We even played as a couple with the Astrups in Madison, Minnesota, and with Ruby and Dick Jackoleto at the great country club in Big Bear, California.

As a substitute for playing the game, Florence would serve as my "drink person" between the seventh green and eighth tee box at our Fallbrook golf course. Our house was situated above these holes, so as I walked down the seventh fairway, I would wave my raised golf club in the air with my cap placed at the end of it. Florence would watch from the deck of our house for the signal and then come down the hill to the eighth tee box and serve us cold drinks! My golfing buddies loved it and would always thank Florence before they continued their play. What a woman!

Christmas Eve family tradition

Perhaps the most crowning event of a happy family serving the Lord happened every Christmas Eve for many years, when we were all together. All twenty of us (our children, their spouses, and our grandchildren) would surprise the whole congregation at the end of the service by marching while singing "Come On, Ring Those Bells," with each one of us carrying a ringing bell, thus closing the entire service for Christmas Eve night. Everyone in the church went home singing that song or had the words to that song indelibly etched in their hearts.

Hostess with the mostest

Our home was always ready for guests. A large dinner was always served after Sunday morning church services; a roast cooked in the oven all morning to be ready for us following the last service. We always encouraged the children to entertain friends at our house, and Florence was always the one to oversee this. Having six people for dinner or sixteen didn't seem to faze her in the least. We may have received this gift of hospitality from our parents. Our parental homes were gathering places after church for nearby farm families, and even the infrequent salesman coming by was welcomed in for a meal. Florence knew just how to serve and make everyone feel at home. I know her daughters and son have learned much from her, as they all love to host parties and dinners for their friends and family. What a hostess! What a woman!

SACRIFICE BRINGS WINDFALL IN TWO WAYS

What could be more fun for my children than to travel to Grandpa and Grandma's in North Dakota? What could be more fun than to have family time in the car, playing "I see, I see," singing songs, and sight-seeing along the way? This was a cozy and fun time for everyone; we were all together in the station wagon, and no one could escape. Great expectations of spending time on the farm, wondering how the horses (especially Starlight) were, how much combining there would be for me to do, and looking forward to great times with the cousins, aunts, and uncles gave us plenty of topics to discuss. These vacations were eagerly anticipated.

After a nudging from the Lord and after some prayerful consideration, I talked with Florence about having her and the kids go to North Dakota this one summer while I stayed behind, as some plans were being made for summer activities at our church. Florence didn't seem to mind going alone, as she looked forward to the time she had with her mother and, of course, staying on the farm where she had grown up. It was tough on me to not go on the train trip with the family. The saddest day was when the family left and the happiest was when they returned after their four-week vacation.

The Lord gave me an epiphany

The epiphany involved extraordinary events regarding our church's confirmation classes for new adult members. Selected speakers were asked to teach. A medical doctor, a doctor of psychology, a counselor for parents and children, and an attorney were chosen to enhance our confirmation classes. Each would take a principle of Christian doctrine and speak about how it applied to their specialty and relate it to the family setting. These speakers were interspersed with my regular classes.

The classes were offered on Sunday evening and Thursday evening and were designed for the doubters and the unchurched. Others were welcome. Many of our members attended, and they in turn met many new people interested in the church. The classes attracted those who were curious to this three-year-old church.

No summer slump for us

Previous summers had full Sunday schools, choirs, scouts, senior citizen groups, youth groups, and other activities going on. We didn't have the mentality for taking the summer off from church. People in our community expected ongoing programs at our church, and it was a great time to reach out and to continue full force in our work for the Lord.

The two confirmation classes had twenty unchurched attendees in each, in addition to our own members reviewing and learning. By the end of that summer, we had forty new members plus children who were baptized and confirmed and some who reaffirmed their faith. A few transfers from other churches were included. One hundred new souls were received into our church membership on Rally Sunday in the fall.

This caught the eye of church periodicals as well as newspapers, as they were curious about how this was done. For the next six years, we had two hundred new members a year join our fellowship. I had mentioned to some of my friends at the time that it was as close to being in heaven as I could imagine. The excitement and the joy overflowed for the Lord from the members of Fruitridge Lutheran (Gloria Dei Lutheran Church).

Giving up a summer work vacation in North Dakota and not being together as a family that particular year reaped many benefits. People were refreshed and excited for the Lord. Seeing families, one after another, with new goals, new experiences, and a new life with Christ was exciting. As the Bible says, "One person gives freely, yet gains even more" (Proverbs 11:24) and "The blessings of the Lord bring wealth without painful toil for it" (Proverbs 10:22). This work was not painful to me, but it *was* like receiving a shot of adrenaline. *Es muss gehen!*

Second windfall

Not only did we have a wonderful response from and refreshment in our congregation that summer, but if I had left, I would never have connected with George Hillestad, a thirty-five-year-old part-time Baptist minister from Arizona. He had come to my church office asking if I knew of any potential salesmen who were in need of a job. I was always trying to find work for unemployed members or friends. He was a distributor for a food-supplement product, which he said everyone needed. He explained more about the product and was sold on it himself. I hardly knew what a food supplement was, as I always conscientiously tried to have healthy eating habits.

I gave him the names of a high-school coach who needed a side job and an old college friend from Moorhead, Minnesota, who had just opened his own chiropractic clinic and needed income. Another man, Don English, came to my mind (Don is mentioned in another chapter of this book), as I really wanted to help out these people, and this was an opportunity.

Being alone and feeling a little sorry for myself at times that summer, I jumped on an airplane and went to Lutheran Bible Institute in Seattle to get in on a three-day seminar on teaching and comprehending the scriptures. As many of us do, I tried to think of relatives and friends to visit during this three-day trip. I decided to connect with Folke Ekblad, a former Swedish Covenant pastor turned Bible salesman and a good friend. He had slept on our couch and shared many nights with our family in our one-bathroom house, so I felt maybe I could spend a night or two at his house. I had heard a pretty good sales pitch on this food-supplement program and thought Folke may be a person interested in augmenting his salary. Seattle was a new market. It would be like opening up a new Ford car franchise in Seattle with no others around. To make a long story short, it turned out to be a great visit and very worthwhile monetarily for him.

Don English and Folke Ekblad took to it like ducks to water. They jumped into their station wagons and went to Southern California to learn more about the product and returned with this food supplement to sell. Being former salesmen, they had many leads. I told Folke that now maybe he could afford an inexpensive motel and wouldn't have to sleep on our couch and hear the hourly chime ringing loudly.

Both of these men became excellent distributors. The owners of the new company even brought them down to the main office in Los Angeles as an extra perk. They had found their gift of selling and were using it.

Each new salesman coming into the business was invited to the monthly sales meetings and encouraged to bring friends. People became sponsors of those they brought in, as I was to Don and Folke. I, in turn, received 2 to 3 percent of what they earned. Don English had group meetings of two hundred to three hundred distributors in Las Vegas, Los Angeles, and other cities around the nation. When he returned to Sacramento, he just itched to introduce me to his many sponsor friends and to tell his story of how this all began. Many looked to him as their hero because he had introduced them to this business.

I had told him from the beginning that I would not permit anyone to introduce me, as I was basically incognito, even though several hundred would see my name on checks and receipts. I told them that I was uncomfortable with others having the knowledge that I was involved in this business, as I didn't want anything to take away from my ministry. Ministry came first! I never sold the product, but I did have it available. I did get overrides from Don's sales, and I received a few thousand dollars each month for a short time. As sponsors, we would write out monthly checks to these men. Florence did most of the work, and we soon realized just how well they were doing and what a successful venture they were in. It made my heart happy to think that I had helped these men and that they were able to pursue this business in this great country in which we live.

A millionaire!
After some years, I came into contact with Don again. By then he owned his own food-supplement business with a laboratory as well as a sales

office. He had thirty employees in his lab alone. I met up with him at his newly purchased home in a beautiful area of Southern California, and he walked me through his past fifteen successful years.

During the next few years, Florence and I were with him and his wife several times, including going out on his two-bedroom, two-bathroom yacht just off the coast of San Diego. Our son, Mark, was attending Point Loma College, situated above the rocky coastline of the Pacific Ocean. We had arranged ahead of time that we would give Mark a signal from this luxurious boat, and he would signal back from his college dorm. His friends would be impressed that his father would be in such a gorgeous craft. I think even Mark was surprised because I never felt I could even afford a small rowboat, and here we were sailing by Point Loma in all of this luxury.

God does provide as we listen and obey Him in our lives.

A MOST EXTRAVAGANT GIFT

Our Sacramento farewell

As an eighth grader, Dorene just giggled as a dear family friend came up to her and said, "I will come to Hawthorne and photograph any of the Hiepler girls' weddings—just give us the word."

This was almost embarrassing to her, but she didn't forget it. She mentioned it to us, and it was in the back of our minds as a most generous farewell gift, not really remembered, as it would be many years into the future before we would accept the gift.

If I hadn't been motivated by an up-and-coming congregation, Fruitridge Lutheran (later known as Gloria Dei Lutheran Church), to begin a Christian day school, I would not have been privileged to serve as principal of the school and to get to know this young photographer and entrepreneur—Bob Loranger and his wife, Laura. Bob called and asked if our school would like school pictures taken. As they had the largest school-photography business in the Sacramento area, I did mention that our school was small and just beginning. That didn't seem to matter. Within a few weeks, he and his wife, who assisted him, were out doing the school photography, and they continued annually and biannually photographing our students for many years.

Bob and Laura had no church

After meeting them, I immediately visited them at their home with the understanding that they were not attending a church. I invited them to come and find out about Fruitridge Lutheran and then to attend our Adult Inquiry class. Bob was unsure, but Laura began attending a Thursday evening class, and after a few weeks, Bob attended the class offered another evening. After attending classes offered at various times, they completed the instruction class and came to the altar, confirmed their faith in Christ, and began a most faithful walk with Jesus for the next fifty-plus years of their lives. I was privileged to baptize their first daughter, and even after we had moved to Hawthorne, I returned to baptize their second daughter and to perform her wedding twenty-five years later. Bob and Laura also traveled to Hawthorne through the years to be the school photographers at Trinity Lutheran; thus, our relationship grew, and we developed into lifelong friends.

The extraordinary farewell gift became a reality for our daughters and son. It came to our minds after Bob mentioned to me that they would be very happy to come and photograph Ilene and Bob's wedding and that, yes, he recalled talking to Dorene some twelve years before. With eight hundred guests attending the Bradberry wedding, Bob and Laura were clicking pictures from every angle imaginable in our beautiful Trinity Lutheran Church. We wanted the best, and the Loranger Studio of Sacramento was it! Six months later, Curt and Dorene were married in a beautiful post-Christmas wedding at Trinity, and Nelene and Jim followed four years later. Fourteen years after Nelene's wedding, Mark and Michelle tied the knot, and guess what? Laura and Bob came with all of their love and expertise to photograph another Hiepler celebration.

After each wedding, I would wait to receive a bill, as just having them come to be the photographers at the weddings was a gift in itself. No bill ever arrived. Laura reminded me again of the conversation at the Sacramento farewell and also at the dinner they had for us the night before we left Sacramento for Hawthorne. This was most gracious and loving of them to do, and it sure saved this poor old dad thousands of dollars for wedding photography.

GOD DROPS WHAT INTO OUR BOAT?

Elmer Vessel's family and mine were trying out Elmer's new boat. Inasmuch as we were leaving the area in a few days, and we could not find a warm night for boating, we went out that chilly night when no one else was out. The six children were all bundled up and enjoying this great boat ride on the river near the beautiful California capitol building under the bridge that leads to San Francisco.

We were all enjoying motoring back and forth when, all of a sudden, Elmer and I looked at each other and said, "Did you notice something fall from the bridge?" We agreed it looked something like a coat. As the evening darkness was fast approaching, we didn't have a clear view of what this was but wondered with some shock, "Do you think that it could be a person?" We were in the area down at the Sacramento River near the Union Gospel Mission, where we had helped out many times, and we thought it could have been a homeless person.

Within seconds, we had put the large boat into high gear and had covered close to a quarter of a mile, circling around the object still floating on top of the water. We immediately sent all six kids into the covered front of the boat in case something dramatic happened.

As we came close to the object, we reached into the water. Sure enough, it was a person. Elmer grabbed hold of an arm, I grabbed one of the legs, and we pulled and tugged until we got the person into the boat. He suddenly stood up, a bit dazed but very much alive!

In the boat the man would not say a word. We noticed he was dressed quite nicely in a suit, with a raincoat over that. He wore a nice watch and good shoes. We headed to the nearest dock and yelled to the man on duty to call the police. They were there in three minutes. Just as the police arrived, my daughter Dorene noticed that he had thrown some papers into the water. Later on, it was acknowledged that these were suicide notes, and they were found near the dock.

I visited him in the psych ward a few times before we moved. He had some personal problems and didn't want to be a bother to his wife and kids. He was the full-time manager of the Sacramento Chamber of Commerce. A pastor friend of mine continued visiting him after we left. He managed to get his life back in order, and for years, he and I exchanged letters at Christmas. He was grateful that the Vessel-Hiepler rescue team was in the right place at the right time that day.

The morning after we had rescued this man, the headlines of the *Sacramento Bee* announced this story. My Christian barber had an interesting comment. "Pastor, some of us work for days to convince people to trust in the Lord as Savior, but according to the newspaper this morning, He [the Lord] just drops them out of the sky into your boat."

CHAPTER 4

HAWTHORNE, CALIFORNIA— HOME OF THE BEACH BOYS AND MATTEL TOYS

ANSWERING A CALL
The following was written by Dorene Hiepler McDougall.

A minister in a Lutheran church can choose how long to stay in a congregation and when it is time to leave. In the early years, a minister would stay five to seven years, depending on how things were going and if he felt his gifts in shepherding a congregation had been exhausted. Due to economic reasons, in the later years pastors have stayed for longer times. If a pastor felt it was time for a move and felt the Lord nudging into a different area, he or she could give his or her name to the church district office, and it would go into a pool from which congregations needing a pastor could select. In many cases, a church may just know of someone it felt would be a fit and would send out a letter of inquiry to the individual. If the pastor showed interest, a process would begin with a time of questions and visits. A thorough background check with psychological tests can also take place before a pastor receives an official "letter of call" to a particular church. The process varies with churches, but this is usually the procedure.

If a pastor shows that he or she has been successful at his or her work by having "grown a congregation," by leading many new people to Jesus Christ, by having had a successful building project, by displaying good leadership skills, by preaching good sermons, and by fostering a loving and caring church environment, this person would never have to worry about not having a job. This happened with my dad. After seven years in Pasco, Washington, and taking this church from a very small church membership to an expanded membership in need of an addition to the sanctuary and a large Sunday school, the Home Mission Board of the Evangelical Lutheran Church contacted Dad about beginning a church in the South Sacramento area of California. This was another new and challenging experience for a thirty-two-year-old, but he was up for the challenge.

In Sacramento, the church grew from just our family to twelve hundred members, a one-hundred-student day school, and two building projects. This was brought to the attention of other churches, and Dad had numerous "letters of call." With God, the sky is the limit. People wanted him. They had heard of his enthusiasm and eager spirit to let everyone near and far know who Jesus is and to preach the Word of God. This came from his desire to be a missionary in China, and now he could do this at home. There were many times I would see my parents in prayer over such a call, asking for direction as to what to do next. This was something that wasn't shared with us children, but if we did ask if we were going to move, the answer was always, "If it is God's will." Of course during the middle of my eighth grade, it was God's will that my dad accept a call to Trinity Lutheran in Hawthorne, California. It was the last thing I wanted to do as an eighth grader because of all my dear friends such as Lynette, Bonnie, Peggy, Jim, Gerald, and Daryl whom I would have to leave! A difficult transition for me! At this same time, a Mr. Michel from Calvary Lutheran Church in Golden Valley Minnesota came for a visit to see if Dad would have any interest in coming to Minnesota. He attended a service and came to our home with a slide show explaining the ministry at Calvary. Dad had explained that he had accepted the call to Trinity but that he had had an interest in Calvary Lutheran from its start in 1946. Dad would go to a Lutheran church just west of downtown Minneapolis to work in the Luther League on Sunday evenings. The Stensruds would welcome him in to their home and would talk to him about a new congregation starting in the western suburb of Golden Valley. Who would have known that fifteen years after Mr. Michel's visit, I would be a member of that congregation in Golden Valley and have Mr. Michel's family as friends. God does have a plan, but Calvary Lutheran was not in it for my parents. Trinity Lutheran in Hawthorne was our next church home.

We had one car for many years. Our good friend Fritz let my mom use his car while he was away from Sacramento. Mom got used to having her own car. During this transition time, Dad thought it would be good to order and purchase a new car before we traveled the four hundred miles to Hawthorne. The car did not arrive! Our transportation to our new home in Southern California was a flamingo-colored Nash Rambler! Picture this: Mom, Dad, my two sisters, and I were crammed into this little vehicle, and oh yes, our cat with her six new kittens was on the floor in the backseat next to our feet! Can you imagine what we must have looked like coming to a new church and home? I'm sure people, such as Rosalind Rosenberg and her mom, plus many others who welcomed us with prepared meals, were wondering, "Just who is this family, anyway?"

Dad was ready and willing to take on the great responsibility of answering the call to this well-established church and school.

Trinity Lutheran in Hawthorne, California

THE MIRACLE OF '61

What would be the most priceless gift a person could receive for Christmas?

Florence and I have been beneficiaries of the most generous gifts from our parental homes, family, and church members through the years. Monetary gifts and food items have always been appreciated, as well as family visits and Christmas celebrations together. I recall, at age four, my parents presenting me with a coaster wagon; a trike at five; and my first Repeater, a .22 caliber rifle, for hunting rabbits and gophers at age fourteen. For my twenty-fifth birthday and graduation from seminary in 1945, I received a 1940 Chevrolet, the latest model that was available at that time. These were all thrilling gifts to receive, but there was still one more at the top of the list!

Gifts of health and wealth are certainly wonderful gifts to receive from the Lord. As parents, seeing our children being kings or angels, or Mary and Joseph in the Christmas play, or seeing them participate in sports and music events, was always a thrill.

Florence and I had been praying for this gift for years

God had His own plan in the timing. Florence was more sensitive and intuitive about this gift than I was. When I tell you what it was, you'll understand why. I knew that our gift would be delivered at a "depot" about five miles from our home. Florence was the knowledgeable one about when we would receive the gift—around Christmas, she'd said.

As many know, Christmas is a very busy time for a pastor, not only in the household but with all of the church activities. Florence had Christmas programs for which she was responsible; she had taught and worked in a kindergarten class since September and had the Christmas program for the class choir concerts and musicals with lights, sound effects, and added stages—quite an endeavor! Christmas Eve brought the traditional foods at home as well as singing and gift opening, of which Florence would take charge. This was always done in between the three or four church services offered that evening. On top of that, our family had a decorating project of traveling around to the various Christmas tree lots, collecting leftover trees, decorating them, and placing them in the chancel of the church for a forest effect for the Christmas Eve services—very festive and beautiful!

This particular year, we returned home from the Christmas Eve candlelight service at midnight. Florence wanted to have our Christmas Day dinner all ready to put into the oven, as we had church services in the morning. Christmas Day this year was also a Sunday. It would be just our family for dinner, so Florence held onto the defrosted turkey as I cut it in half, as that was all we needed. Pumpkin pies were ready for the oven. With services and choirs singing the next morning, this all needed to be ready to shove into the oven before church services. It would then be ready when we returned at noon. (Florence would run home in between services to check everything.)

The "Centinella Depot"

At about 5:30 a.m. Christmas morning, Florence had a "special feeling" that our gift, for which we had prayed for so long, might be delivered at the "Centinella Depot," more commonly called a hospital! That Christmas morning, December 25, 1961, at 7:00 a.m., our gift arrived. Nelene, nine years old; Ilene, twelve years old; and Dorene, almost sixteen years old, woke up to notes taped on the cupboard giving directions on how to prepare everything for the Christmas dinner, as Florence would likely not be there to supervise. Florence had left great directions for the girls. They all did their jobs and waited excitedly for some news via telephone. About 8:00 a.m., I popped in the door to announce the arrival of a brother, born about an hour before.

Florence and I had literally jumped into the car at about 6:00 a.m. that morning and quickly made our way to the hospital. Florence disappeared for forty-five minutes while I waited in the waiting room at Centinella Hospital. A nurse appeared in less than an hour with the news that our treasure, our miracle had arrived. A couple of minutes later, the nurse arrived with a large red Christmas stocking filled with our son. I was filled with excitement and emotion. When I finally saw Florence, we chose the name Mark Orville Hiepler for our son. What a Christmas gift!

As I said before, we had prayed for another child and would have been happy with another girl; however, after having five sisters and no brothers, three daughters and no sons, it was good to welcome a boy.

There was a 10:00 a.m. Christmas Day service at which I had to preach, so I hurried home with the announcement for the waiting girls, and then on to church we went. Dorene helped with the choirs and did a good job with the music for her mom. I have never been happier in delivering a sermon for our congregation than when I could tell them what had happened that morning. They couldn't believe it. Many had no knowledge that we were expecting, as in that day it wasn't talked about. Florence also said that she didn't want to worry anyone. Doesn't that sound like Florence? It was more personal than in this day and age. I told the congregation in the announcement that this morning the male population of the parsonage had increased to two—some thinking I said *by* two, so happy sighs and some groans were heard throughout the church. Florence was very discreet with her fashions. She had two black sheath dresses for which she eventually let the darts out and had two or three different jackets that she wore over top. Around the church on Sundays, she was always dressed in a choir gown, so most had no idea that she was expecting a baby. Even after this Christmas announcement, some thought that we had adopted a child.

Spiritual birthday
New Year's Day was the following Sunday, and that was the day Mark was baptized—on his seventh day of life. That life, implanted by the Holy Spirit, was witnessed by parents and sponsors on Mark's baptismal day and nourished and renewed at his public confirmation in eighth grade. His Word says that "you must be born again by the water and the Spirit (John 3:5). Just as we as parents gave him his physical life without his knowledge, so God also gave him spiritual life through the Holy Spirit in holy baptism. What a miracle of '61 for Florence and me!

AN EXTRAORDINARY PASTOR'S WIFE
Some call her "phenomenal." Other adjectives to describe my wife are helpful, confident, caring, faithful, godly, counselor, volunteer, teacher, Mom, Grandma, Great-Grandma, and much more! Many of our

friends have expressed these feelings after moving away and finding pastors' wives are not all the same.

She not only directed three choirs on Sunday mornings at times, but our home was a place where people she invited could receive new hope for their life, their children, and their marriage through her God-fearing ways.

Her spirit of helpfulness was so extensive that she would drop everything she was doing if someone came to the door needing help, counseling, or just an opportunity to talk. Everyone knew she would listen. She was the type of person about whom everyone who knew her would say, "She will give you a real lift if you are down." This wonderful spirit would often be fulfilled by being available to people she had led to Christ and nurtured through our Evangelism Explosion program. She was one in the first team of four people that I trained once a month, three hours at a time, for three months. These teams would go out with me calling on new people interested in knowing Jesus and our church. One team would go out on Wednesday evenings, and one would go on Thursday mornings.

I had trained with Pastor James Kennedy at the Coral Ridge Presbyterian Church in Fort Lauderdale, Florida. On the departing day of the weeklong training, Pastor James would say, "Now, don't expect your wife to be one of the evangelists on your team back home in your church"—unless your wife is Florence!

She was always ready for another challenge.

Florence was the best at sitting down in a home with her two teammates visiting with the interested person. She would inquire about the person's interest, whether it was in our church, Sunday school, or elementary school, and she would show a deep love and interest in that new person's life.

Florence had led one such person, a woman, to Christ. Both she and her husband took the Adult Inquiry class and become members of our church. She did not immediately become the perfect saint! She had many problems that surfaced again and again. It wasn't unusual for her to call Florence once a week for advice on how to raise her children, what to do with rebelliousness, and how to have harmony in a family and marriage.

The woman's stress hit her hard one day, and she just dropped everything, jumped into her car, and started driving. She called Florence periodically through the day, reporting to her that she was OK during this flight/drive throughout L A, Burbank, and the Glendale area. Florence kept her calm and kept her talking during each conversation, eventually talking her into explaining where she was, what area, and down to what telephone booth she was calling from.

We were scheduled to go to California Lutheran University for the homecoming parade, where our daughter, Nelene, had been chosen as the junior princess to accompany the homecoming queen for the festivities. (The following year, in 1973, she would be the homecoming queen.)

We decided that we would follow through and find this woman in the Burbank area, about a forty-mile trip, and then go from there to Thousand Oaks for the festivities. I am always eager to save gasoline. In addition, Ilene and Bob were going with us to Thousand Oaks. Here we were, going to search for a woman in an unknown area, who was suffering from stress. What would we find?

"All things work out for good to those who love the Lord and are called to His purpose" (Romans 8:28).

We found this fine lady in a telephone booth on a certain corner, but she was in no mental condition to drive her own car home, so we invited her to come with us to homecoming, after which we would be going home. One small problem was that she had a car that wasn't in the best condition, and there was no place to leave it. It was still an hour's drive to Thousand Oaks. Guess what? Bob volunteered to drive her old clunker ahead of us all the way to Thousand Oaks. She rode in our car next to Florence, feeling safe and secure, and all of us did enjoy homecoming. This woman received the best guidance imaginable by having caring people such as Florence be there for her. She also experienced a Christian family working together and experiencing happiness together as our family modeled. Good came out of adverse circumstances.

Bob drove the car ahead of us on our hour trip back to Hawthorne. Our friend lived nearby and was united with her anxious family, and we never heard of any other major problems. She is still a good friend of ours. Her husband had been a fun golfing partner, even after we had each moved to other areas. He influenced me to go to more than one of the great golf tournaments at the Riviera Country Club or Rancho in LA. He went home to heaven a few years ago.

I got in contact with our friend a few years back. She told me to tell Florence she had finally quit smoking about three years ago and is most happy in having no desire to smoke again. She said, "I know this will make Florence even happier."

Believe it or not
While shaking hands good-bye with hundreds on the last Sunday at Trinity Lutheran, our friend came to me and said, "We are planning on buying your house because we love it so much." They had many happy years living there.

Things of this sort happened over and over again in our ministry, and Florence deserves the credit. This is my Florence.

OUTSTANDING CHURCH MUSIC GROUPS

What do you enjoy about church music groups? Let me share five things I feel are important.

1. Music enhances spiritual growth for individuals who sing praises to the Lord.
2. Music increases church attendance, fills empty seats, and impresses new attendees.
3. Music encourages each individual to praise the Lord more regularly in a beautiful way.
4. A children's or youth choir assists parents in getting their children to church, rain or shine.
5. Music builds confidence and not egotism through a unified, governed group serving every week and not just talking about serving.

For a few years, all twelve months of the year, I was blessed to see six choirs every Sunday—two choirs at each of the three Sunday morning worship services. Each choir chose songs that fit the church year or at least the theme of that Sunday. We expected at least 175 singers each Sunday, plus family and friends.

With God's help, I was also fortunate in finding committed and talented choir directors. The greatest find of all was Florence, who started several junior white-robed children's choirs; a red-vested boys' choir; a larger choir that had tryouts; a red-robed children's choir made up of forty kindergarten children; and the confirmation choir of the seventh, eighth, and ninth grades. Florence also shared her talent as a participant in the adult choir.

In addition, you'll read in the following chapter about our fabulous traveling concert youth choir. I've asked Jane Skuba, John Brewer, and Pastor Ollie Olson to share about our youth group and concert music history at Trinity Lutheran in Hawthorne.

I didn't know what God had in mind
The following was written by Jane Skuba.

The year was 1970, school had started a week prior, and our son was officially a kindergartener. This particular morning, I was at home with our two-year-old. I began a messy project of stripping 1940s wallpaper from one wall of our small two-bedroom house. Our daughter was very much entertained watching Mommy.

Midmorning, as I considered a break from my project, the doorbell rang. With gloves on and a scraper in hand, I blew back the string of hair from my face and opened the door. "Well, good morning," said the well-groomed man standing on the porch. It was Pastor Hiepler, along with his parish education director, Elda Leslie. (I can still hear pastor's cheerful voice saying, "Well, good morning.") In years to come, I'd hear that same voice say, "Well, good morning" many times, but on this day, he continued with introducing me to Elda, and then he said, "We're calling on parents of new children attending our day school this week."

I invited them in, removed my gloves, and picked up our daughter as we sat down in the front room. We must have talked for an hour. The time just flew by. Pastor was the most sincere person I think I had ever talked with. Elda was also a delight. (She was one of the best parish education directors at one of the largest ALC congregations and day schools in the South Pacific District—Trinity Lutheran Church in Hawthorne.) I told my husband how pleased I was by their visit. That next Sunday we attended one of Trinity's church services.

We didn't know what life-changing experiences God had in mind for us the day I decided to remove old wallpaper. Now, almost forty-five years later, I think how blessed our children were to attend a wonderful Christian day school and a wonderful Christ-centered church like Trinity Lutheran. We had the opportunity as a family to listen to Pastor Hiepler every Sunday. To this day our son says, "The man I most admire and trust is Pastor Hiepler. He never preached to us; he showed us by example. Through all these years, he has been the most honest man I've ever met."

Under his leadership, our children learned to be leaders themselves. Their value system was cultivated in a loving, Christian environment. They learned to respect others. They attained academic excellence and values that have helped guide them in their careers even today.

It was a wonderful time, but life was not perfect. Financially, it was not always easy to keep our children in a private school. There were sacrifices and trade-offs. Buying a new car, a boat, or a motor home was out of the question if we were going to pay tuition. Even a second job was sometimes necessary. Most years our family didn't vacation. A weekend trip now and then had to suffice. Those years may have been the first "stay-cations" (stay-at-home vacations), but God provided.

Our children were our priority, and their foundation was most important to us and worth the cost. We can say the nurturing of our family's faith and the grounding of our foundation has made life a journey full of blessings. God is good.

Our children never knew their own grandfathers but considered Pastor as a grandfather figure in their lives. Of course while Pastor was a major influence in the lives of many children, his wife, Florence, was always an ever-important presence, leading and teaching countless children over the years. Both Pastor and Florence always made everyone feel accepted.

Looking back, I joyously recall the bicentennial musical directed by Florence. There were at least two hundred children who participated. The musical was called *I Like the Sound of America*. The children were all dressed in red, white, and blue and stood onstage with the most enormous American flag as a backdrop.

Obtaining the flag is a story in itself. Mary Lou and Bev, two dedicated Sunday school volunteers and day-school moms, stopped at a local car dealership where this huge flag flew proudly every day and asked the owner of the dealership if they could borrow the flag for the musical. He was impressed that they would work so hard to help make the bicentennial musical so special that he graciously agreed. It took several men to load the flag into the back of Bev's large station wagon. The car immediately sunk low to the ground from the weight. When they arrived back at school, it took several men to take the flag out. One can imagine the teamwork involved. Who knew a flag that big would weigh so much! Due to the enormity of the flag, when it was returned to the car dealership, the local fire department even brought their ladder truck to assist in attaching and raising it again.

I lent my modest artistic talent to design and draw the front of the musical's program, which included an American flag. Many other parents pitched in to help. Why did they help? Why did we help? We rallied around Pastor and Florence to help provide the best for our children, just as parents had done before then and for many years thereafter. We all knew that Pastor and Florence were providing the best Christian guidance for everyone with whom they came into contact. We were blessed to be a part of those efforts.

Pastor had the children's choir sing on Sunday mornings, and Florence directed each of the youth choirs: the children's choir, the boys' choir, and the junior choir. Our children were in all of them at one time or another. Whether a sermon or a song, there was always a Gospel message that flowed out of the voices of these children.

Both of our children were married by Pastor Hiepler, and his wife, Florence, sang at their weddings. Like countless others we've known, our lives are richer today because of Pastor and Florence's dedication to reach others for the Lord. We need more dedicated men like Pastor. No matter what time of day or night, Pastor has always been willing to help one in need. I remember one late night when Pastor knelt in our front room with our family in prayer. I'm sure he has knelt in countless living rooms and has knocked on doors or rung thousands of doorbells during his vast ministry. He has always been a true shepherd.

Just a few days ago when my husband was recovering from knee surgery, Pastor Hiepler once again rang our doorbell. This time he carried in dinner. We were so blessed that evening by his visit, and the hamburgers were good too.

At ninety-four, he is still serving others. I am humbled by how genuine he is, and I pray God will someday raise up another like him. Pastor Hiepler has spent his life sharing the Good News of Jesus, reminding us of the scriptures, "The gift of God is eternal life through Jesus Christ our Lord" (Romans 6:23) and "For by grace are you saved through faith; and that not of yourselves; it is the gift of God, not of works lest any man should boast" (Ephesians 2:8–9).

Thank you for the opportunity to share a brief glimpse of our past with the Hieplers and God's amazing hand in all our lives.

The following is a copy of the program from this performance:

I Like the Sound of America, by Flo Price

America has a nice sound doesn't it? It's a word that means a lot of different things to different people. To the Rev. Samuel Francis Smith who wrote "My Country 'Tis of Thee," it was "rocks and rills" and "woods and templed hills." (I can't believe I've lived so long without knowing what a "rill" is! Webster's says it's a small brook.) If you look around you, it's no wonder another songwriter got carried away and called it "America the Beautiful." It is. To many other people less poetically inclined, its meaning is very down to earth; "Mom, the flag, and apple pie." Whatever it means to you, I think you'll agree with me that it's a pretty great place to live.

Now about our junior musical: First of all the kids had fun doing it—right from the beginning when they found some "goodies" in an old trunk in the attic and began to try them on and wound up having a parade. (Guess I've never grown up—I'd still do this if I had half a chance!)

But, disguised under an old army helmet, a worn out bugle, and some of the other treasures, lie some pretty basic and important truths about liberty, freedom, and what has made our country great. And most important of all, the kids learn that in order for a country to use the motto "In God We Trust" and really mean it, each one of us has to personally trust God—individually, for himself—and that's about as basic as you can get.

By the way, don't wait for the 4th of July or other patriotic day to practice patriotism. It can be done any day of the year—any time you feel the need for a little flag-waving. I think it's high time we did some, don't you?

So have fun friends and please toot the bugle just once for me, will you?

Flowers were presented to Mrs. Hiepler tonight in appreciation for endless dedication to our youth choirs.

Coordinating Committee: Mrs. Robert Fagent, Mrs. Walter Lusk, Mrs. Bill Martin and Mrs. Peter Skuba.

CHARACTERS

Steve Corona, Robin Aasness, Paul Arnold, Richard Misenheimer, Mark Korshavn, Nancy Jordan, Colleen Martin, Stephen Fenske, Jack Weise, Lois Leslie, Albert Gunderson, Dana Hansen, Mark Hiepler, Monte Miranda and Brian Norden, Barbara Jerde, Debbie Brandt, Tammy Mathias, Patty Noah, Linda Crizer, Judy King.

Living proof music ministry (1972–1978)

The following was written by John Brewer.

In 1971, life was pretty simple for me. I was twenty-nine, married, and had two daughters. A third daughter would come later. I had a good job in aerospace and was paid a fair wage. Basketball, softball, and the piano were a few of the things I enjoyed playing. Oh, and I sang bass in our church choir at Trinity Lutheran Church, in Hawthorne, California.

There was one particular Thursday night choir practice that I'll never forget. My life changed that night. Looking back, I can see clearly now that God began implementing a very special plan for me. I was about to begin a seven-year outreach mission, which involved leading a large group of people who were being charged with winning many souls for Christ.

That particular Thursday night, our senior pastor, Orville Hiepler, was there at the beginning of rehearsal. He brought us the sad news that our choir director had suffered a heart attack and would not be available to direct us for some period of time. Pastor asked if there might be a volunteer from within our choir who would be willing to fill the gap—at least for a short while. After much prompting from my "friends" in the choir, I accepted the challenge. Why? Well, little did I know, but the journey had begun.

You should know that I had never directed a choir, had no training on the subject, and didn't really have a clue going in. I did have a good appreciation and some knowledge about choir music, however, thanks to a mom and dad who made sure of it. God had also blessed me with other talents, which were about to be put to use (and to a test) in a big way.

After a couple of months, our director had sufficiently re-covered and returned. It was then that I was invited to direct the high-school choir of about twenty-five youth. I accepted. I was enjoying this directing thing and had always loved working with youth.

In 1971, another thing was happening at Trinity. Our youth group was beginning to flourish under the leadership of our youth pastor, Ollie Olson. The youth were coming in large numbers on Friday nights with Bibles in hand to listen to this man of God teaching in his gifted manner.

One day, Pastor Ollie invited me over to his house for a chat about the youth ministry and how music could potentially play a greater role. He shared a book with me that contained the music and words to a Christian folk rock musical entitled *Tell It Like It Is*. He also handed me the accompanying record of the musical being performed (to be played on a record player). He asked if I would be willing to evaluate the package and gauge whether or not our own youth could learn such a piece and whether or not they'd accept the challenge.

After a week or so, I returned to him with two answers: "yes" and "yes."

This was the beginning of an outreach ministry unlike any other Trinity had experienced in the past. In looking back, this entire ministry ultimately consisted of a number of servants being choreographed, used, and directed by God to spread the Good News of Jesus Christ. I found myself living inside a miracle. There is simply no other way I could describe those years.

The youth loved the musical and learned it. They memorized every note and word of every song. It was presented in the spring of 1972 by our group of sixty-six young people, mostly Trinity youth, but with a few friends also in the ranks. I believe it was the Holy Spirit that motivated our youth. Something fun and very special had been presented to them. They knew it, and they felt it. They were excited about recruiting other young people to join and did so in amazing numbers. We would come to understand that in doing this, many souls would be won for Christ.

That spring, *Tell It Like It Is* was presented three times in Trinity's Parish Hall, as well as to Hawthorne and Aviation High Schools at special assemblies arranged during after-school hours. The Word of God and the message of salvation were being presented, and the Holy Spirit was touching lives through our kids.

It had become clear to Pastor Ollie and me that this had become both an "in-reach" and an "outreach" ministry all in one. The lives of so many of our own youth were being changed. Those who heard the musical were clearly blessed and wanted more.

By 1973, the number of singers had grown from sixty-six to seventy-eight when we presented a musical entitled *Love*. We added a small accompaniment band of six youth as well as some footlights, overhead lighting, drama, and more complete choreography. In addition, volunteers built risers for the kids to stand on.

Living Proof shared the musical *Love* at a number of churches in the area, as well as the Naval Training Center in

San Diego, the Terminal Island Prison in San Pedro, and three times at Trinity, and it concluded at El Camino College.

Enthusiasm couldn't be stopped

I believe it was in 1973 at one of our Saturday evening performances at Trinity that it began raining midafternoon. Since the event was indoors, we had no problems going forward with it. We did, however, anticipate a smaller audience as a result of the rain. Well, all of our performances at Trinity were standing room only over the years, but this particular Saturday evening, people came prepared. Many brought their umbrellas and stood outside in the rain, watching through the windows. Those early days were special to us all. God was using the kids in ways we had never expected. What a joy it was to watch the Holy Spirit at work in so many lives.

In 1974, I introduced the group to another new Christian musical entitled *I'm Here, God's Here, Now We Can Start* at our January retreat. Living Proof had grown from 78 singers to 112! We also enlarged our band to ten members and added ten adults and youth who took care of all production needs. This included music equipment, instruments, risers, overhead and footlights, and sound! My dear friend at Trinity, Fred Noah, led all things technical for Living Proof. Fred recruited and trained others, who became valuable contributors.

We decided to establish an evangelism team in 1974 from within Living Proof. The team decided to distribute prayer request and comment cards along with the programs. The cards were collected after every performance. Our Living Proof Prayer Team would go over every card and bring any prayer requests before our entire Living Proof team for group prayer. We continued receiving letters and other correspondence. I personally responded to each one. This had become a significant ministry in three short years—and oh, how exhilarating!

In 1974, our planning team had decided to take the youth to San Francisco via chartered buses, where we presented the musical to a few churches along the way and to other churches in San Francisco.

Camp Pendleton in San Clemente was added to our itinerary in 1974. That door was opened by a wonderful chaplain with whom I had numerous conversations. The number of marine recruits who heard the message of salvation each year was huge. Camp Pendleton was truly a wonderful harvest field through the years, as we watched the Holy Spirit transform the lives of many young recruits who were at an important crossroad in their lives.

Before winding up, I would like to provide you with a visual of the Naval Training Center in San Diego. It's a very large naval base housing many young men and women who represent many different faiths. Each year when we went there, these groups combined their individual weekly worship services into a single, large service to hear Living Proof. We sang in a large auditorium with an upper and lower deck. The floors were all wood—no carpet.

From 1975 through 1978, the Living Proof ministry continued to flourish at Trinity under the inspiration and guidance of the Holy Spirit. Our Christian musicals were presented to an estimated twenty thousand people over time, many of whom dedicated or rededicated their lives to Christ. What a blessing to us all!

Neither Pastor Ollie Olson, who presented the idea of a youth musical to me entitled *Tell It Like It Is* in 1971, nor I, the contented twenty-nine-year-old youth choir director, could have imagined how far-reaching this ministry would become.

God took us into places and in directions that we could never have imagined. It was an honor and privilege to be a part of every minute of this ministry.

In closing, I want to share that some of our kids went into full-time ministry for the Lord as pastors, missionaries, and musicians. Others went into teaching in Christian schools or serving God in other ways. I know that every member of the Living Proof team had a life-changing experience during those years, and that wherever they are today, they are indeed being Living Proof to all of God's boundless love.

John Brewer has been a great friend of mine and a leader at Trinity Lutheran Church. He is truly a man of God. Thank you, John, for sharing about another of the great ministries at Trinity in Hawthorne.

Largest Banana Split in All of Southern California

We started a bus ministry in order to reach children whose parents were not committed to bring them to church on Sundays. We knew such children would benefit considerably when they found out that people in that church on 130th Street cared for them. A group of up to eighteen people would spend two hours on Saturday mornings going door to door within a ten-mile radius of our church, asking if parents if their children could be picked up the following day to attend our Sunday school.

Pastor Pinke and Mr. Dean Holen were the directors of the six buses that picked up the children and then delivered them back to their homes on Sunday mornings. One of the bus ministers, Dr. Shelby Thorpe, told me in 2014 that she has stayed in contact with one of the students from an "unchurched" home. The follow-through each week with a phone call on Sunday morning before pickup and having a special church service and Sunday school for these 250 children was quite a ministry in itself, as we already had five hundred in regular Sunday school. This showed these children that we cared for them and their souls. Shelby said this person was still an active Christian in a Lutheran church near Knott's Berry Farm in LA. Even after thirty-five years, we see "the Word of God does not turn away void." (Isaiah 55:11)

Bushels of bananas and six busloads of kids!
As a special treat one Sunday, the children had ice-cream banana splits. These were not the usual kind from the Dairy Queen. Their spiritual taste buds were delighted in Sunday school and their stomachs fed.

Mr. Dick McAndrews, a contractor and president of our congregation who was building our adult ministry center at Trinity, made possible the largest banana split that any of us had ever seen. He furnished over two hundred feet of commercial building troughs used for water run off on large buildings. These new, unused, immense troughs were carefully prepared and reached around our large educational building with cement blocks for everyone to sit on. Gallons of ice cream and a pickup truck full of bananas and toppings were furnished. The 250 children, bus ministers, and Sunday school teachers all sat next to one another eating out of this trough. I was privileged to join them in the banana split feast and then share a spiritual message of joy and rejoicing that these children, having first received the wealth of food in Sunday school, were now receiving a thank you from the church for being a part of our program. We trust that the Lord's wonderful love may pass on from generation to generation so that the words of Jude 1:21 may be fulfilled: "Keep yourself in the love of God, looking forward to eternal life."

A Prairie Farm Boy Now on Mayor Yorty's Task Force

I never sat at his right side nor did I ever become a close friend with Mayor Yorty or his successors, but I at least was able to be in one of the tallest buildings in the city once a month for a few years. Mayor Yorty welcomed all of us into his office and celebrated with us yearly at a special picnic for senior citizens. He was always open to many of our suggestions as well. We may have thought of ourselves as unimportant people from the suburbs of LA, but he made us feel needed and welcomed our input.

My congregation may have felt that our church was more influential in the city when their pastor, in his forties, was chosen to serve on the mayor's senior citizen committee to help make the city a greater influence for good. This could have impressed them, especially that the mayor and committee would choose a man who was the senior pastor of a known larger church simply dedicated to reaching souls for Christ and strengthening the Christian work on the way to heaven, preventing some from being on the road to hell.

I did have the opportunity to be the invocation leader at the city or county dedications and assemblies. It did not hurt my opportunities to be called in for leadership in some otherwise secular gatherings in our own smaller communities.

Just going up into that city hall building for a committee meeting in one of the largest cities in the United States would never have entered my mind twenty-five years before. God is full of surprises!

HURRY, HE'S TRYING TO KILL OUR YOUTH PASTOR

Our youth pastor was somewhat new to our church. He came with good recommendations, as he had been the youth director in one of our most successful churches in the LA area. His relatively new wife was also a very dedicated, active participant in her husband's youth department and in all of his interests. We felt fortunate to have him on our most successful team, which was now composed of about fifty-nine part- and full-time paid servants of the Lord. I personally had a double interest in his success—first, because I wanted us to have the best youth director

anyone could find, and second, because one of my own children participated in the youth activities.

I came into the common reception area of my office and the offices
of the youth director, the pastor of evangelism, and the pastoral principal of our five-hundred-student elementary school. The general secretary and receptionist had a separate open area with a counter where
people were served. As I came into the office one day, all seemed to
be very ordinary except for the well-dressed young man sitting there,
waiting for our youth director. As I gave a friendly greeting to him and
welcomed him into our office, he offered hardly more than an imper-
ceptible nod.

I went into my office at the end of the hall next to the youth director's office. After about thirty minutes, the youth director came in,
after which I heard some loud talking and shouting. The youth room
was immediately above my office on the second floor, so I credited the
noise to the youth. However, minutes later the receptionist buzzed me
and said, "Hurry—that well-dressed tall man is trying to kill our youth
director!" I left my office immediately and looked into the next office.

I saw this man on one side of the desk striking vicious punches at
the youth director, who was ducking rather effectively from most of
them. At the same time, the man was yelling, "I want to kill you!"

All I could do was distract him from his goal while the receptionist
called the police. I grabbed his arm and pulled him around, trying to
give his victim a chance to get away. I yelled at him to stay out, keeping
far enough away myself—after all, I had been a track star, not a boxer,
and I wanted to avoid becoming his victim. The intruder continued to
yell at the youth director, "You stole my girlfriend and married her. I
hate you!" It was a good thing he had no weapon except his fists.

Our youth director finally scrambled out of his corner and ran into
the school secretary's office at the other end of the hallway, only to be
cornered behind another desk in that empty office. The man threw a
few more punches at the youth director, with me pulling his arm and
staying out of punching reach, and the youth director, now even more

out of it from the battering he had received, jumped over some chairs and ran out to the open playground with the intruder right on his heels. About that time, the police arrived, handcuffed him, and put him into the back of the squad car.

We helped the youth director bandage his bruises and cuts, while thanking the Lord that it was all over with no more severe results. You can guess what the group of people that had gathered around were wondering.

This young intruder had apparently dated the youth director's wife some years earlier. He was the son of a prominent couple who lived in Hollywood and who, incidentally, were counselors in a high school and a college. However, what happened to them could happen to anyone, as their son had started on drugs rather young and had even been in a drug recovery program but had all of this hate tied up inside him.

Soon after he got out of jail a few days later, he threatened the youth director again. The result was that the youth director and his wife had to leave our church and move into safe isolation for some time. We certainly hope that this guy eventually received some help with his life.

On the lighter side, one good thing came out of this event. My son, Mark, an eighth grader, was overjoyed that day at how his popularity had soared, as the kids really enjoyed seeing his dad "beat up on the guy that wanted to kill our youth leader." In that situation, I certainly got more credit than I deserved.

SCARY, UNBELIEVABLE!

The secretary called me in my office two doors away and excitedly said, "A caller just told me a bomb will explode at our school and church within the hour!" Sixteen teachers and about five hundred children were moved, within three minutes, out of the classrooms and into the farthest corner of the playground.

There was no principal in the office at just that time, so I pushed the button that allowed all sixteen teachers to hear my voice. After it was all over, I asked the teachers if they'd believed it was just a regular fire drill. They said the only clue to the fact that it might have been something more was that I was so calm.

The SWAT team came and spent an hour searching for some indication that it was real. Apparently, an eighth grader who had been expelled for a couple days was the guilty one. He had used a lower, disguised voice when he made the telephone call to the school.

Marriage: Two Extraordinary Dreams Come True

Two distinctly different desires through childhood and the teenage years became reality by marrying the right man.

Ilene, our middle daughter, would ask almost every Christmas, "Is this the Christmas that I can get a pony?" Of course she knew her mom and dad desired to give her every good thing that would make her happy, but her wish did not come true.

We lived in the city with reasonably small lots, and our finances were never that plentiful, but she continued to ask with a quizzical smile, knowing it was almost impossible. "Do you think *this* year I could get a horse?" We would try to appease her requests by taking her out to Napa Valley Ranch Club, where for a yearly membership of ten dollars we could horseback ride as a family. Even Florence rode. She had grown up on a farm and helped with outside chores, but she had never ridden a horse until then. At times while we were in Hawthorne, we would occasionally spend a day off in the Palm Springs area. Early in the morning, Ilene and I would go horseback riding, and then later in the day, we would do some activity that involved the whole family.

Summer vacations were spent in North Dakota. I would help with combining for my dad and make enough money so that we could purchase a reliable car when needed. At the same time, Florence would take the children to her parental home on the farm in Tioga. There her brother and wife, together with his children, Corrine and Juris, would have horses ready for "those California girls" to ride when they would appear for a two-week farm experience. This is when Ilene fell in love with Starlight, a beautiful, fast Shetland pony. The love of horses was in her blood from Grandfather Gustav.

Ilene had felt a deep, sincere desire to be a teacher since junior high school, and she went on to attend California Polytechnic State University. She met a young man at Cal Poly whom she had known in high school at Lutheran High, and she invited him to a Campus Crusade gathering on the university grounds. In later years, while speaking in our church, Bob said that he never expected that the young lady who invited him to go with her to a Christian gathering would be his wife three years later.

We jokingly said to Ilene, "We know why you married Bob—because his dad has horses." The Bradberrys lived near Will Rogers State Park, so riding those trails with Bob's dad or other family members was a dream come true for Ilene. Some years later, on her fiftieth birthday, Bob Sr. gave her his horse and, later on, another one for his son. Unbelievable! A dream did come true.

Bob finished his education at Cal Poly in San Louis Obispo and an additional year in Florence, Italy, receiving his very-much-treasured degree in architecture. Ilene also took a fifth year and received her master's degree in reading education.

Mission dream comes true

After one year of working in their trained fields, with promising careers, they gave it all up. At this time it was Bob who had a longing to go into the world missions "somewhere in the cosmos." Somehow, almost simultaneously, both received a very deep longing to answer the call to begin work with the Agape Mission program of Campus Crusade for Christ. They were sent to Swaziland, South Africa, to lead a school and to teach.

Florence and I were very happy to think that our son-in-law and daughter would go into the full-time ministry, but we were sad they would be so far away. Florence and I were privileged to visit them twice in Swaziland and Zimbabwe. My sister, Ruth, and Florence traveled there at another time. Their commitment was for two years. Fourteen years later, they returned to the United States.

Missions prepared Ilene and Bob for a challenge
Bob and Ilene used their talents and experiences from the years in Africa and joined the staff and ministry of a small church in Southern California called Saddleback Church of Orange County. Did I say small?

This congregation has fifty thousand people attending on holidays, and at this time they have a number of satellite churches. They also do outreach around the world. Bob became an ordained pastor along with forty others and works with the PEACE program focusing on Rwanda. Bob has become as important in Rick Warren's successful Saddleback Church as John the Baptist was in Christ's ministry. Ilene, in turn, is using her gift of teaching English in the ESL program of the church and programs in Rwanda. In her spare time, she is an adjunct instructor in English language at Concordia College in Irvine, California.

Oh yes, she is also using her love for horses, as she and Bob have a small group from church for those interested in equestrian experiences.

God is wonderful! In one way or another, He has fulfilled and honored Ilene's wishes and dreams. He promises that "as we trust Him, He will give us the desires of our hearts" (Psalms 37:4).

May our desires grow through the years to be in His will.

USING HER GIFTS

Whether it was for the love of playing the piano or some gentle insistence from Mom and Dad, Dorene played for the fifty-voice, white-robed children's choir every Saturday morning practice and every Sunday morning service. Not only that, but during her first years in high school, she played the flute in the school band and frequently on Sunday mornings.

Our first daughter, Dorene, didn't have it easy, as we expected her to attend church at least once on Sunday morning and Sunday evening, Wednesday Bible study, and prayer. We always expected the best from her in how she acted and what she did. She regularly attended Luther League and became president for a year as well. The main social group she enjoyed coming home to during her college days was the College and Career group at church. Her best friends, Geraldine and Darline, were an integral part of the College and Career group. It also helped that she had some interest in a fellow in the group.

Being our first child, she did not have much of a choice as to where she would go to high school. We strongly believed in Christian education and, I'm sure, made her think that *she* had chosen Lutheran High School of Los Angeles. The only negative was that the school was eight miles away and cost $1800 a year; the education outcome, however, was great. She had four years of fantastic teachers, made many friends from all parts of the Los Angeles area, was part of chapel every day, and participated in other activities in the school, such as band, choir, and Melody Makers. During her senior year, she was chosen as the drill team captain, which included being a drum majorette. She led twenty-five girls in routines at football games and participated in parades, while the drum major led the marching band. We were proud of her at the various sporting events, maybe more proud of her than the quarterback's parents were of him.

Dorene was quite a social person, and two rules we had for her dating were challenged many times.

The first rule we had was no dating until age sixteen and then only if well supervised. The second was no steady dating until out of high school. As I said, we were a bit rigid with our first child.

I would like to share with you some of the values that were extraordinary or even unbelievable in her thinking, especially regarding influences from home, parents, and school. Here is Dorene's "take" on things.

As I look back, I could not feel more privileged to have been born into a family such as ours. Yes, there were rigid rules that didn't make sense such as curfew at 10:00 p.m., even though I was out on a date and the movie wasn't over until eleven; or having evening meals together and, of course, Sunday dinners.

I sometimes had important things I wanted to do with my friends, like go to the beach, or "drag" Hawthorne Boulevard, or go to the Wich Stand for cherry Cokes, or meet with friends at Denny's, or go to Twenty-Sixth Street in Manhattan Beach and just hang out with Ger and Dar, my best friends! As I look back now, I see the value of many of these rules, as we needed family time together, and meals were our time to communicate with each other. I was a bit of a rebel and needed boundaries.

At this time, being a "pastor's kid" was an identity for me. We were watched and spoken about, so we needed to always be an example, which was our role, as our dad was the pastor. There were some pressures, but also some good guidelines for me to follow. I needed them to an extent.

In talking with friends who also grew up in pastors' homes, I found that many felt neglected by their dads, as they spent so much time with their parishioners and not enough with their families. This was *not* the case with me.

It was called *time management*.

As a family, we would accompany Dad on hospital visits, waiting in the car while Dad made a hospital call, knowing that after the visit we would be going to William Land Park to play or to Bridgeman's for ice cream or many times a picnic in the park. There was time to play catch or play croquet together (the balls and mallets were always in the trunk). We would have "family night" on Friday nights (when in elementary school) and would have "game night" or have projects such as "paint by number" with oil paints. Making fudge and pulling taffy were some other great moments. I remember coming home from college and observing that after evening dinner, Dad made sure that he had even a fifteen-minute time frame to play catch with Mark before he headed off to an evening meeting. Dad always made sure there was time spent with his children and made use of every spare minute.

As I mentioned earlier, our identity and our lives centered on our church family and church life. My best friends were made through our church and school, and they have remained lifelong friends. Many of my friends today will comment to me, "You know so many people—how is that possible?" Having moved to three different communities during adolescence, and the church being a common denominator, how could I not have so many important people in my life?

Traditions were emphasized strongly and became a norm, especially at holidays. Dad would bring up the German traditions, but because he grew up in a Scandinavian community, he was familiar with *lutefisk, lefse, krumkaka,* and *rummegrot,* which my mom was an expert at fixing. My grandmother (Dad's mom) made the best Scandinavian meals, even though she was born in Germany and spoke with a strong accent, because they were surrounded by Scandinavian settlers in North Dakota. I have tried to carry on these food traditions in our family and with my children.

What a great privilege it was to be born to my parents, who gave me so many opportunities and made a strong Christian home and church the center of our lives.

From Her Lips: "It Is Terminal"

I was on a trip from our home in Hawthorne, California, to Chicago, Illinois, and had decided to stop at the Mayo Clinic in Rochester, Minnesota, to visit my sister.

It was a very busy time in my life in 1961. I was in need of an experienced, trained, and committed pastor to lead our already-growing elementary school and Sunday school. We saw the greatest potential I had ever known. I had been in Hawthorne only over a year. We had a wonderful principal who was also a full-time kindergarten teacher at our school of 250 students. This was before we had our preschool. I had worked on all of the state requirements and gotten them in order, and we were ready to buy a house next to our church property for the preschool. However, Miss Esther Olson, the principal, had decided to move and work in a different area. Pastor Hiller, whom I had known at seminary as one who was more mature than the average student, had been a public school teacher and administrator. He had also been the editor of a newsletter to all pastors of our denomination. I had followed his successful work after seminary, and he looked like a good candidate to fill this position.

Pastor Hiller came to California for a challenge, and he met it by directing our day school and Sunday school with great and optimistic leadership. He and his wife became such good friends of ours that we asked them to be sponsors for our son, born Christmas Day, 1961.

All of the reasons for making this trip were dwarfed and almost forgotten when I made the stop in Rochester. There was a reason God told me to stop there that day: so I could be there with my sister to hear her say these words: "It is terminal." My sister Gertie told me in the first ten minutes of our visit that the doctor had just told her the treatment he was prescribing would only prolong her life two to three years more, if it worked. I was grateful to be with her at this time but shocked and saddened to hear this news. She was a wife and the mother of three children in their most formative years. Gayle was in the sixth grade, Gloria in the eighth, and Glenn had just completed high school. Gertie had had surgery in Williston, but the cancer had gone into her incision, and it was not healing. The good news was that she could at least leave the Mayo Clinic and go to the comforts of her own home.

Nothing right now was more important to me than to be with her for the next couple of days, especially until she could get back to her home with her caring husband. Gilly and Gertie's family had been living in our old family home about twenty miles from Williston (the town to which our parents had retired). Gertie was cared for by the doctors there. I immediately canceled my flight to LA and rented a car so I could be with Gertie for the next couple of days and help Gilly so he didn't have to make the seven-hundred-mile trip to Rochester. I changed my flight to leave from Williston a few days later.

In the next two days, I had many thoughts that I had never had before. Our immediate family had never experienced terminal illness like this. Our family was intact. My mother was only sixty-eight and Dad seven years older at this time. Gertie was the oldest and the one we all looked up to. She was a "farmerette" and had been my sixth-grade teacher, and I had lived with her and Gilly during my junior year in high school in Epping. She was a kind, gentle soul and a great support to her family. She was more than a sister—she was a pal.

We talked, cried, prayed, and even laughed occasionally. We shared all of the good times we had had together when still at home with Mom and Dad. Time passed quickly on this seven-hundred-mile trip.

She expressed how she loved her family very much. Her dear children were precious to her and to all of us. Gilly had always been such a right-hand man on our farm even before he and Gertie were married. He would help my dad fix all of the more delicate things that needed the work of a mechanic. In later years, he did plumbing and electrical work, and he was trained by his dad as a garage mechanic in our small town. Gilly wasn't just good; he was the best you could get! Our parents were helpful to Gilly and Gertie, obtaining a couple quarters of land for them,(a quarter is 160 acres)which is still in their family. Gertie, Gilly, Mother, and Dad did so much for each other through those years.

We went immediately to their home on the farm after our long trip. Very soon after I left, Gertie went to live with our parents in Williston to be close to the doctors and immediate medical help when needed. She experienced our parents' tender care.

As I was leaving, we prayed again for a miracle of healing for her, and I was expecting to come back to see her the next summer. That didn't happen; I came back in only a couple of months for her funeral. Even as I write this, I am sobbing like a baby, as she meant so much to me and to us all. Every time we went back home to Williston, we missed her so much! We do have the sure hope of heaven for her and for all of us who love the Lord. This Bible verse could be called a key verse in this book of faith and hope for the future and all eternity for our families and for the families of Glenn, Gloria, and Gayle: "For I know the plans I have for you; plans not to harm you, plans to prosper you and plans to give you hope and a future" (Jeremiah 29:11). When we are in heaven together, we may understand why she was taken from us.

Gertie and Gilly gave Florence and me a plaque for Christmas a few years after we were married. It has hung in our home for years, witnessing to the many who have gone through our doors.

"Only one life, 'twill soon be passed, only what's done for the Lord will really last."

CHAPTER 5

CAMARILLO, CALIFORNIA— RURAL AND SUBURBAN LIFE

The following was written by Bev and Carmen Lusk.

PRAIRIE BOY'S LIFE IMPACTS FIVE GENERATIONS

"How great are His signs and how mighty are His wonders!
His Kingdom is an everlasting Kingdom and
His dominion is from generation to generation" (Daniel 4:3).

How does a young prairie boy from North Dakota influence five generations of one family from California? It seems a bit farfetched, but that is exactly what Orville Hiepler has done through his love of the Lord, love of family, love of people, and love of his country. His love for the Lord stretches farther than his arm span, wider than his smile, and brighter than his eyes.

Our family's path crossed that of Pastor Hiepler's in 1960. Helmer O. Ekern, a Norwegian farmer from Houston,

Minnesota, moved to California with his wife, Georgia, in 1946 to be near his daughter and family. In 1949, they joined Trinity Lutheran Church and became very involved in ministry. It was in this role that he was appointed to the deacon board, which in 1960 extended a call to Pastor Orville Hiepler. At this time, Pastor Hiepler was serving Gloria Dei in Sacramento, California. Pastor Hiepler accepted the call to this fifteen-hundred-member congregation. This was his initial introduction to the first generation of our family. Pastor and Helmer became very close while serving the Lord and continued to build the congregation. In addition, they felt God leading them to expand the Christian day school. Through this strong belief in the power of Christian education and his community outreach, Pastor Hiepler immediately began to bring new families into the church. This was an exciting time in the life of Trinity Lutheran. He believed in Christian education, which brought young families in the church and youth to the Luther League.

Amazing wife

As we all know, a pastor can serve his congregation well, but behind this pastor is an amazing woman by the name of Florence Hiepler. Pastor's ministry would not be what it was and is without her. Since young families were joining the church, there was a great need for a youth choir. Florence served as choir director for three choirs. She gave of her time and talents, which God has blessed her with. She rarely was seen on Sundays without her choir robe. Her spiritual encouragement and partnership with her husband in ministry blessed Trinity Lutheran beyond measure.

Helmer and Georgia's daughter, Helen, married Kenneth Kling. They were faithful members and had been nurtured in their faith through many men of faith, including Dr. Gaylord

Falde and Pastor Andrew Anderson. Through his deep desire to serve his Lord and Savior, Kenneth took a more involved leadership role under Pastor Hiepler. Pastor Hiepler recognized Kenneth's leadership ability and his willingness to serve. Kenneth served two terms as congregational president, accomplishing many large projects under Hiepler's tutelage. The vision for beautifying God's house was without limits. Stained-glass windows were installed, as well as bells for the empty, soundless bell tower, new carpeting for the thousand-member sanctuary was acquired, a building was added for adult ministry, and large iron gates for an interior patio were just a few of the beautification projects. These iron gates were placed by Kenneth in honor of his three daughters, Bonnie, Beverly, and Barbara—the third generation. Kenneth lost his battle with cancer and entered not through iron gates, but the heavenly gates in 1979. This example of service by Kenneth and the encouragement of Pastor Hiepler laid a foundation for many generations to come. Pastor Hiepler and Kenneth had much in common—their German heritage, their love for the Lord, and their love of family. They valued who they were in the Lord and who they were in their families.

"Train up a child in the way he should go: and when he is old he will not depart from it" (Proverbs 22:6).

The mission of training up a child in the way of the Lord continued to strengthen and expand the Christian day school. Kenneth and Helen Kling's daughters all attended Trinity Lutheran Christian Day School. Under Pastor Hiepler, it became the largest Christian day school in the South Bay Area of Los Angeles, having almost five hundred students, with two classes for each grade. The key to the school's success was the shared vision of Pastor Hiepler and his associate pastor, Sherman Korshavn, seeking excellence through a Christ-centered school. Many of these children were unchurched; however, almost every family who placed their children in the school desired to become members. Pastor Hiepler made each family feel very special. His ability to serve each family as their shepherd was a gift from the Lord that God saw in that boy from the prairie. This ministry through Christian education was not contained within the walls of the classroom. It became a community out-reach, spreading the Gospel throughout neighborhoods.

As mentioned, Kenneth and Helen had three daughters. Beverly, the oldest of the three, married Walter Lusk. Walter began serving on the church council as a school-board member and eventually as school-board chairman for many years. Beverly and Walter's four children all attended the school. Pastor Hiepler was not only a spiritual leader in the church and school, but he was a father figure and dear friend to Walter and Beverly. He baptized and confirmed all of Walter and Beverly's children: Kristin, David, Jonathan, and Daniel.

Camarillo, a great future life

In 1976, Pastor Hiepler felt the call to First Lutheran Church in Camarillo, California, about an hour north of Hawthorne. For several years, several families traveled from Hawthorne to Camarillo on special occasions to attend church services. Palm Sunday was one of those in 1980. Following the service, these families spent time with Pastor and Florence at their home. They always made you feel like you were part of the family. On this visit, one of the family members had said, "It would be fun to live here." Next thing they knew, they were in Florence's car on their way to a new housing tract to look at model homes. End of story. Six months later, the families all had moved into a housing tract called Woodside Greens—five families, following the Lord through the love of their pastor and spiritual leader.

Walter, a leader in the church

Now in Camarillo, Walter acquired many of his leadership skills through the mentorship of Pastor Hiepler. The foundation of Christian leadership Pastor has instilled in Walt by being a living example has served Walter well as a husband, father, and in the workplace. He also unselfishly gives to his community and serves with a joyful heart. Without hesitation he encourages you to give of yourself to others and serve your community by being the hands and feet of Jesus. In this way, Walter has served on the Camarillo Planning Commission for many years and is still serving today. At one of the heated commission meetings where Walt was serving as chairman, someone asked him how he was able to keep the meetings under control. He said, "Oh, that's easy. I learned it by watching my pastor handle church council meetings." Pastor Hiepler has continued to serve his church and his community, being an example to not only Walter but to all generations who have been blessed with his leadership and guidance.

In 1980, Beverly and Walter were confirmed as members of First Lutheran Church, Camarillo, where we all became active members. They have raised their children in this church where they were taught God's Word, not only by preaching but by Pastor Hiepler's Christian example of living God's Word. He taught them and laid a strong Christian commitment in their lives and hearts. They have taken this Christian wisdom and teaching into their career and homes. Even to this day, they still rely on his wisdom and consider him their pastor and shepherd.

Walter and Beverly's oldest son, David, has turned to Pastor Hiepler many times for spiritual guidance and advice. David served as a police officer and detective for sixteen years. At one point, David was injured on the job and was medically retired. Shortly after, David felt the Lord's call to attend the Association of Free Lutheran Theological Seminary in Plymouth, Minnesota. With much prayer support and spiritual guidance, Pastor Hiepler was influential in his decision to follow the Lord's leading. During the process of David feeling God's call to ministry, there were many who were skeptical; however, one who was not was David's wife, Carmen. Carmen also was blessed to have had Pastor Hiepler as her pastor, being baptized and confirmed by him. Many times, when Satan allowed doubt to enter their minds regarding the call, they would turn to Pastor Hiepler. One night, just days away from moving to Minnesota, they sat across Pastor's dinner table. Pastor and Florence both spoke of how proud David's grandparents (Kenneth and Helen Kling) and great-grandparents (Helmer and Georgia Ekern) would be. David and Carmen will never forget seeing tears roll down Florence's cheeks as she recalled the generations that had come before and the love they had not only for the Lord but for their family. To have that reassurance and encouragement from them meant more to David and Carmen than they can put into words. David is now in his last year of seminary training serving as an intern. During these training years, Pastor has encouraged them through his phone calls, letters, prayers, and encouragement. It is their prayer that Pastor, the man who baptized and confirmed, encouraged and mentored, will be present to participate in David's ordainment.

His influence in this family continues on. This is now the fifth generation. All the Lusk children are all married and have children. Kristin and Michael, married by Pastor Hiepler, have three children, Ashley, Jay, and Carley; David and Carmen have two children, Jacob and Olivia; Jonathan and Wendy have three children, Nathan, Nikolas, and Ella; Daniel and Cynthia have two children, Garrett and Russell. This fifth generation has been blessed to know and love Pastor Hiepler. They are so grateful to have been able to experience his love as a shepherd. Pastor Hiepler's life speaks to the fact that no matter your age, you never retire from serving the Lord and can do it with a joyful heart. He considers it a privilege that the Lord has more for him to do.

Pastor's influence on our family spans the generations. His joyful heart reaches out and touches the lives of those around him. His love for his fellow man is insurmountable. Pastor Hiepler will be there whether you need him to be your rock in times of doubt, your comforter in times of sorrow, your shepherd when you feel lost, or your cheerleader when you celebrate. He will be there, no matter the hour.

The following is an excerpt from a letter written to Jacob Lusk by Pastor Hiepler on his confirmation in 2012.

Jacob, we, who have been a part of your life through your parents, your grandparents, your great-grandparents and your great-great-grandparents, are thrilled and appreciative of your taking this important step in your life, confirmation. I can almost hear from heaven your great-great-grandparents, the Ekerns, and your great-grandparents, the Klings, saying "Thank you Jacob for standing firm in your faith." It has been my privilege to know your wonderful grandparents on both sides and to have married Walter and Beverly 49 years ago. God has been so good to you in giving to you a rich heritage. Being I love you and will pray for you, I become your Cheer Leader in that you have set a good example also in studying, in commitment, and in confirmation. May I share with you three great cheers: 1) Cheer of Forgiveness: "Be of good cheer, your sins are forgiven." 2) Cheer of Companionship: "Be of good cheer, it is I, be not afraid." 3) Cheer of Victory: "Be of good cheer, I have overcome the world."

Five generations now look back over their shoulder to see what a boy from the prairie of North Dakota has accomplished. It is only fitting that this prairie boy became a shepherd for the Lord. Once Pastor

Hiepler is your shepherd you are his sheep, a part of his flock. He and Florence will always care for you, no matter where you are, and more importantly, you know he's there for you if you need him. It is our prayer that God will bless your life with a spiritual leader, mentor, and shepherd like the one that was called by our Lord and Savior from the North Dakota prairie to serve His Kingdom on earth.

CHRISTIAN EDUCATION

Some call it extraordinary—having two jobs in one

My advisors recommend that I include in this book anything considered extraordinary or anything that will help other people serve the Lord more extensively and more completely, and this seems to me to be one of those stories.

I had the great privilege of being in the right place at the right time to become the principal of the Christian elementary schools. In Sacramento, one loyal and faithful kindergarten teacher, Mrs. Dotty Halberg, was principal from 1954 to 1960. Our school had grown to a K through eighth grade at that time with exactly ninety-nine students. I had been the founding pastor in 1953 of Fruitridge Lutheran Church in the southern part of Sacramento, California. We had great leaders in the principals at Trinity, and it continues.

Camarillo grades K–8

While already having a busy parish at First Lutheran in Camarillo, California, the congregation and I decided to start a kindergarten in 1982, with a plan that we would add a grade a year. I served as principal, with all of the daily jobs, as well as doing the long-term planning, selection of teachers, and the promotion of this school to all of the surrounding area. About four years later, we felt able to support a principal-teacher so that the volunteer principal in the form of the senior pastor of the congregation could assist in starting up a New Ventura county high school. Mr. Newman, a credentialed, well-experienced, and committed man of God, moved with his family from Orange County to our school. We had just reached a student enrollment of 144 with five full-time teachers, three part-time teachers, and a fourth and fifth grade. From that point, Mr. Newman carried on an ongoing expansion of joyful participants. Our focus was to reach the "down and out" with scholarships and the "up and out" with the best academic education possible on earth as well as a strong Bible- and Christ-centered emphasis. It is believed that the four medical doctors' families and a layman's family who all joined the church at that time were greatly influenced by our school.

Below are the words of Mr. Newman presented at the school dedication:

At First Lutheran School, as we begin to move forward in our program of education, we want to make sure we have laid the proper foundation; that we have built the solid school not made of wood and nails but rather the chief cornerstone, Jesus Christ Himself! That's the basic goal of our school, to bring children and parents into a lasting and growing relationship with Jesus Christ. He's the foundation, the "concrete" in our program. The solid base. [As stated in 1 Cor. 3:11.]

Once that foundation is in place, the rest flows out of love for the Savior—the history, the phonics, the math, the reading, and English, helping children who struggle and to answer parents' questions.

For a Christian day school to get started and remain strong and healthy, good leadership is most vital. It's been said over and over again in Lutheran school circles: "Without a senior pastor who supports, nurtures, and loves the Christian day school, it won't endure." This senior pastor championed the cause that was dear to the whole church—a school where Christ is the focal point, where He is glorified throughout the school day.

Jog-a-thon 1985

Christian Day School Groundbreaking

I can't believe how fortunate I was to lead this school for the first four years! It served as a great way to reach every person who inquired about the school with the Gospel and information on our church. It was fun for once in my ministry to serve as principal-superintendent of a school when my family didn't attend, inasmuch as Mark had completed high school and was in college by this time. As a parent I had "been there, done that" and now could look at the school from a different perspective.

People would say, "You must really love Christian education, or you are a fool to serve full time in two jobs." My answer has usually been that I would like to see all of our Lutheran churches with schools. I was so thankful for a smaller Missouri Lutheran Church school in Kennewick, Washington, where our first daughter Dorene attended first grade. Bus service over the river into our neighboring town of Pasco each day was such a help. Dorene had a great foundation for learning.

Almost every church has a school

"Train up a child in the way he should go and when he is older he will not depart from it." (Proverbs 22:6). I truly believe that a great benefit in Christian day schools is that what we teach at home on a daily basis can be followed through in the classroom as well. When we plant the seed at home as parents, these Christian teachers can continue educating with Christian values as well as the reading, writing, and arithmetic.

A building with our name on it? Unbelievable!

The church council and congregation at Good Shepherd bestowed on me this great honor of naming the South Building the Hiepler Building. What a generous, kind, and undeserved gift! Guess I was at the right place at the right time as a former pastor of First Lutheran (now called Good Shepherd). I had been pastor there from 1978 to 1990. This was a very alert, motivated congregation ready to move ahead. They eventually needed more space and a new building, which has taken the Hiepler name. New programs were activated and the school enlarged, and great outreach was underway.

While it was being built, it drew the attention of all of our Lutheran churches in the neighboring cities from Santa Barbara to Thousand Oaks. This is depicted in an accompanying picture of thirteen pastors and three laymen. Two of the laymen were members Ken Graham and Dr. Donahue. Dr. Miller, the president of California Lutheran College, was our main speaker, and Pastor Don Solberg of our national church body participated in the dedication of this new building of eight classrooms for our Christian day school.

MIRACLE AT ARNEIL ROAD

Twenty years later

This happened in 2009 and 2010 at First Lutheran Church and Good Shepherd Lutheran Church in Camarillo, California. As the Lord guides me in using five or six names (of the others who were involved), He may also show others in our congregation or in another church what great individual leaders the Lord provided when leadership was needed. "Glorify the Lord with me. Let us exalt His name" (Psalms 33:3). "I sought the Lord and He answered me. He delivered me from my fears" (Psalms 34: 4).

I am on the bright side of ninety—closer to His eternal glory. I happened to be in the right position in relation to both congregations so that no other person could be as neutral as I have been. First, I had been a pastor for eleven years some twenty years earlier at First Lutheran, at which time we experienced a high peak of life and growth in that church. The kindergarten-to-sixth-grade elementary school with six teachers and a principal was a blessing. We also had one of the largest building programs in First Lutheran's history, which was the South Building. Furthermore, we added a second full-time pastor who was the youth director. As a matter of fact, the last thing I was privileged to witness was in January of 1989, when the congregation dedicated the new pipe organ (almost all paid for at the time of dedication). This $67,000 purchase is now worth more than twice that price. This all indicates that our congregation was healthy in the area of growth and in the development of stewardship.

The key phone call in God's miracle-working grace

Late on a Friday night, Walt Lusk, the president of the First Lutheran congregation, called and left on my answering service information that no one else except two of his closest friends knew. I couldn't believe what I heard: there could be a possible merger between First Lutheran and Good Shepherd Lutheran Church.

The day before the call, Jane Skuba, Bev Lusk, and the vice president, Brenda Cook, of First Lutheran were all 100 percent involved in this great conclusion. Pete Skuba and Rick Gulbranson made and seconded the motion to talk with the president and pastor of Good Shepherd and to consult with me about the possibility.

Many months before, I had written to the church council of both congregations and had suggested a merger of the two churches. I told them that I would be happy to serve as a mediator or coordinator of what had to be done. I received an official letter of thanks from the First Lutheran Church Council saying that they were relatively happy in the new synod of which they had been a part of for a few years. The surprise then came in that they were now ready for a merger of the congregations.

First, I had to contact the congregational president of Good Shepherd Church, Brad Shaub. I approached Brad and posed the question to him that since the congregation was thinking about acquiring property or having a permanent home, would they be interested in receiving property worth several million dollars that already had a church building and a school building? As he was a professional businessman, he held back his excitement, but he did answer that such an offer would be hard to refuse!

It was also very natural for me to share the good news with my son, Mark, who, next to Florence, is my closest friend on earth. He was also an elder at the church. He, from that time on, was of great assistance in making everything come together for the two churches. My daughter-in-law Michelle, an attorney, was the next person I made fabulously happy by telling her the news. She had been on the council at one time, and the church was most fortunate to have an attorney on their council. Who wouldn't be thrilled to have a volunteer legal advisor?

The Lord's hand was seen all over these negotiations. When we found it necessary to make the final step legal, so many extraordinary things happened. The Lord had planned this uniting of Good Shepherd Lutheran Church and First Lutheran. Pastor Johnson was a natural to come into a situation where you had next to no staff, no facilities, no traditions, and everything was up for grabs. The church, which had been growing under good leadership for a few years, was ready for more growth. Good Shepherd had developed a positive reputation even though it was meeting in many temporary locations, such as schools and office buildings. I shared the good news with Pastor Johnson, and he wanted to remain neutral. Meanwhile, I had his full approval to go ahead with the project on the part of both congregations.

Two great presidents and an attorney made it go. Another good president was elected at the annual meeting of Good Shepherd. As a matter of fact, the new president, Michael Drews, and Walter Lusk aided me later with a congregation in Sacramento that needed some help. These two men, in my estimation, were God's men in God's place at a vital time in bringing the two congregations together. Mark and Michelle were also key people and held the first meeting of the two congregations at their home. By coincidence, it was my sixty-fifth ordination year as well as our sixty-fifth wedding anniversary, so everything was celebrated. The merger of the congregations would officially take place eight months later at 380 Arneil Road in Camarillo.

Florence and I loved going back to Camarillo twice a month, which we did for about six months. We drove 165 miles for each of those trips. We would attend Good Shepherd at the early hour and First Lutheran at the later hour. We had so many good friends at both churches. Also it was a pleasure to be with Mark and Michelle and our three grandchildren twice a month.

In June of 2010, Pastor James Johnson from Good Shepherd came all the way to the hospital in San Diego twice while I was recovering from my serious surgery. He also thanked me for the part I'd had in bringing the two churches together and asked me to speak, if I was well enough, at the dedication and consummation of the work we had done to make the merger possible. The Lord provided the strength and even the caregiver to make that possible in September of 2010. I was extremely thankful to God for what He had done and for the great opportunity He had given us in being the Lord's servants at this important event that many friends have called a "miracle of God."

I felt that this happened to show people the reality of John's words in 5:24: "Verily I say unto you, whoever hears My word and believes Him who sent me has eternal life and shall not be condemned but is passed from death to life."

The ultimate goal is to reach more people with the Gospel.

CHAPTER 6

OCEANSIDE, CALIFORNIA, AND FALLBROOK, CALIFORNIA— AVOCADO CAPITAL

A NEW APPROACH TO STARTING A CONGREGATION

The Oceanside church property was truly a *godsend* to us after meeting temporarily in two different schools for two and a half years. During this time of organizing and growing our church, our home in Fallbrook became an adequate facility for all midweek meetings and as the church office. Our living room served as a beautiful place to have a wedding. Florence always served as a "hostess with the mostest." Our home was about seven miles from the Oceanside site we had chosen for our new church.

After two and a half years, we had hit a plateau in growth and enthusiasm. We continued looking, asking, and praying and found a fine facility that was being vacated by the Evangelical Free Church in a strip mall on East Vista Way in Vista, California. We'd even had a funeral in the facility, and all plans were ready to move in.

Apparently, the Lord had better plans for us because another church that was looking for a facility got their foot in the door ahead of us, and it was rented to that church instead. I drove up and down the street in an area off Mission Road looking for "For Sale" signs that might lead us to the right place for us to expand our new growing church. We were ready to rent or buy almost anything. However, having no accumulated building fund or a reputation where banks would gladly give us a loan, we had no equity in anything. But we *did* have the need, faith, and enthusiasm to try almost anything. *Es muss gehen!*

A house was finally found
We found a house that had been vacated and could be used temporarily. I called the realtor who had it listed, and we looked at it together. It was only a half-acre, and the rule of thumb was that we should have two acres. On our second trip to look at the property, I asked my friend and church member, Jim McMillen, to meet with us there. As the three of us stood up on this hill looking over the beautiful view of the valley in Oceanside, we spotted a rundown, shabby, debris-filled lot just below. As we took a closer look, we could see two old cars, three unkempt buildings, and discarded refrigerators lying around. The three buildings were so bad that they all should have been torn down. There was some retail and commercial property fronting Highway 76 on this all-inclusive property of 5.7 acres; I could see it was a big fixer-upper and lots of work. The average person would have looked at it and said, "Oh no, let's please see something that at least looks better."

We also noticed that three families lived on the premises in the two dilapidated trailer houses near the main buildings and also in a small house (some would call it a flophouse). We learned that ten years before, a man had acquired the property as a possible shelter for the homeless and maybe a small church and private school. All of those projects had begun to take shape but came to a screeching halt when this man (a reclaimed street person) died in 1990, just a couple of years prior.

Even though this man who had accomplished some of his dream had died, his wife and her daughter and grandchildren continued to live in a small part of the church-school building on the campus. The principal of the school lived in the main house and tried to keep it open for the street people. They were all working to make the best of the situation. By this time though, everything had gone to wrack and ruin. The elders of the site were a couple who lived in the only nice home on the property. After we spoke with them, they were happy to think that a church was interested in the site and that the mission could continue, even if in a different form.

If you don't buy it, we will

I asked two of my former trustees from Trinity (who were now living in the San Diego area) to give us their opinions on the property. They were already more than sold on the fact that the property was well located. It was in a mixed residential area of apartments and lower- and high-priced homes and conveniently situated off Highway 76, not far from a developing shopping center. This also had investment potential for us; we could sell an acre of view lots and still have ample room for parking and building a new church. My experienced and truly successful friends walked the whole property more than once with me. Each of these longtime friends—Burton Friestad, a realtor in Fallbrook, and Noel Hand, who was not only a builder but also an owner of apartments and other properties—said if we didn't buy this, he would. Both men wanted this property for our developing congregation. Our focus would be on children and youth, replacing the former emphasis on the homeless. The elders and former owners were delighted to visualize our plans for the property.

Four of us continued the dialogue with the owners and followed up with negotiating until we finally had a consensus on the final cost of the property at $405,000. The real-estate market was at a low in 1993, and the elders of the property had a real need to sell. We had a great need for expansion. It was a wonderful coming together for all of us.

No down payment—miracles happen!
We had no building fund and no "deep pockets" that we knew of, but we did have a deeply committed, 100 percent unified, unselfish, and positive new congregation of forty family units for a total of one hundred souls. We had just organized a few months prior and assured the main church body of the Association of Free Lutheran Churches that we could do it on our own. They were more than happy that the fourth church in California in three years was about to be built.

The Lord gave us a new concept and approach at this time. We called it "Investors for the Lord," inviting our own membership and relatives and friends to make loans to our church at 5 percent interest. We assured them that should anyone need their money back—whether it be five thousand, fifteen thousand, or forty thousand—sooner than the agreed time, we would honor that request. Gifts flowed in from friends who weren't even members. One friend, Fritz, had been generous to all of our congregations and gave a major gift at this time. Another woman who had been on one of our tours shared her wealth with this church as well as the Association of Free Lutheran Churches Seminary in Minneapolis. A few needed early repayment, but they were quickly replaced by other people eager to make a loan to us. All fifteen who were involved were paid back by 1998. The Lord, in turn, was right there to give even larger gifts.

We, of course, had some bumps in the road, such as a partner-developer who was not truthful and held up some of our progress, but that issue was soon settled. This was a great disappointment but taken in stride.

The many shared Saturday workdays on the new property imparted a sense of ownership, accomplishment, and fulfillment for our members. The camaraderie that these folks built among themselves was a real gift for our new Community Lutheran Church. With ads in the paper telling others that old trailers, refrigerators, and pieces of wire and metal were for sale, we cleaned out the property and put in new playground equipment. Remodeling the building used for worship was also a great accomplishment brought about by our faithful members working in their spare time.

The Lord further authenticated this purchase a few years later when a visionary and hardworking new member found a buyer for 1.1 acres for over a million dollars. We all praised the Lord. Today those lots are filled with beautiful family homes. We retained our buildings and three acres with beautiful view lots.

It has become our church. Miracles do happen!

Q: How do you play 107 holes of golf in a day? Quickly!
Eighteen energetic players came to play a fund raiser at the Vista Shadow Ridge eighteen-hole golf course. After renting the entire course for one day, we had a golf cart for each player and a bucket of extra balls in each cart. We finished our breakfast and morning devotional and teed off at 6:30 a.m. Excitement was all around, as most of the players had never played more than thirty-six holes in one day, and that had been a record. To think we would try to play over one hundred brought smiles and determination to all our faces.

We did not stop for lunch but received a lunchbox, which we could nibble at while another player was hitting the ball. There would be plenty of time to eat later. Water bottles were abundant and would be handed to us without us coming to a complete stop.

Even though we were competing against each other and played by most of golf's rules, we could only look for a ball for one minute and would not be penalized for a lost ball. We always played "ready golf." We also asked the one who was ready to putt out and then move on to the next hole and tee off. We didn't feel hurried, but we did save all of our visiting until the six-thirty dinner when our wives joined us.

Most of the golfers were from our church, and a few others were from San Diego and Northern California. Bob Gately was from Bakersfield and was also the one who raised the most money for our new church children's club, the Pioneer Club. His $1,800 included "hole sponsors" for him. He played 110 holes, and the group averaged 107 holes that day. This meant he had used a lot of shoe leather while contacting many of his friends in Corcoran and Bakersfield. It also meant he loved children and loved golfing almost as much. His wife, Margaret, came along and cheered us on at every turn. This couple returned to the Oceanside church many times to visit with new friends they'd made at this golf marathon in 1993.

We had men like Jim McMillen, who served as a perpetual gopher, attending to everyone's needs. He must have had a leg- or backache that day, as he was an avid golfer.

Fifty children benefited from the marathon

Mrs. Shirley McDonald led the Pioneer Club for our children from the church as well as the neighborhood. Well-trained teachers were excited to be a part of this program, which was held midweek after school. The $12,000, minus expenses, that was raised by the marathon was the best golf money most of us had ever spent and was a great experience! We prayed that every part of this most vigorous day would serve the Lord and that, through the Pioneer Club, children would know Jesus.

Sky-high jump

At the end of a service, Community Lutheran Church in Oceanside, California, experienced the fulfillment of a promise. I was so enthusiastic about the surge of attendance on Palm Sunday to 120 from an average attendance of 90 that I could hardly even stand it! The new church had been in operation for only two years. I was so excited that I told the congregation, "If our attendance next Sunday shoots up to 140, I will stand at the door and give the 140th person a fifty-five-dollar study Bible." It happened. The 140th person had a wife and three children, so it was a gift to the whole family.

During the service, I'd said that I was so thankful and elated over the increase in attendance that I could "jump sky high." Ten minutes later, I started speaking to the whole congregation from the roof of the church. I told them that the "sky-high jump" landed me next to the steeple, so I hadn't quite reached the sky, but I got close with the help of the ushers and the stepladder.

This was the first time that so many raised their heads looking heavenward or steeple ward, rather than bowing their heads to receive a benediction.

What Do I Do Now?

New and renewed excitement, adventure, and success after the age of seventy

I had several motivations to keep me active during my seventies: to be worthwhile; to help other people; to serve and glorify God's name; and to help others financially, as the Lord had provided for me. Thus began my involvement and travels with the Campus Crusade for Christ.

Ages 77–79: two one-way trips to Siberia

Jokingly, my friends called them "one-way trips to Siberia paid by my church." Seriously, the trips were paid for by the church, Community

Lutheran, as they thought it was an act of benevolence and something that they could give to me, since I had been their pastor as a volunteer for ten years.

The twenty-eight other people from the United States on the trip were a great side benefit; otherwise, I would never have been the recipient of their above-average attitude in service to the Lord, which was the highest priority.

This program in Tomsk, Siberia, was a part of a program started by the Campus Crusade for Christ. It began shortly after the fall of Communism and freedom from the orbit of Russia's direct influences.

It was one of the most far-flung and strategically timed opportunities to introduce the influence of Christ to teachers and administrators in their public schools, showing them how to teach the Bible. It was an antidote to the great increase in crime and juvenile delinquency in the entire old Soviet Union.

I was privileged to teach for the days that we were there in Tomsk, two thousand miles northeast of Moscow. Tomsk, Siberia, was a city of five hundred thousand people. The others in the group were placed where they were qualified to teach and where they were needed. I had already had the experience of being a principal at our church schools in Sacramento and in Camarillo for a total of ten years, and in Hawthorne, California, I had been senior pastor for seventeen years and the superintendent for the school at Trinity Lutheran.

Tomsk is a city of apartments
Concerning the city of Tomsk, the weather was around zero degree Fahrenheit on the days we were there—both times during the month of May. California people had told me how I should wear extra layers of clothing and then take them off as necessary when inside buildings. Having lived my first twenty-five years in the northwest corner of North Dakota and gone to college and graduate school in the more northerly part of Minnesota, I didn't find that temperature unusual for the winter months but a little unusual for the month of May. As was

typical under Communist Russian influence, they had a good educational system and a very well-controlled way of managing it, so the teachers and the administrators all had a good education, even though not one of the 160 attendees had a car. One teacher I'd met on my second trip had married a guy who had a very little car: being a tall person, I had a difficult time getting both legs inside it.

Well-dressed on thirty dollars a month

The teachers were all well dressed, even stylish in the eyes of people from the West. My daughter Ilene pointed out that they wore the same dress and shoes day after day while we were there. They had been saving up their thirty-dollars-a-month salary to look good when the Americans came.

People in general appeared to be healthy, maybe because they walked every place they wanted to go or stood outside waiting for public transportation. They had rather efficient buses and taxis. Perhaps they got exercise walking up and down the steps in their apartment buildings—very few had elevators. During both visits, I was never in what we would call a house—everyone lived in apartment buildings. It was usually a matter of whether someone could afford one- or two-bedroom living quarters. Many apartments were basically one large room.

What is an instantaneous translator?

The people were not only friendly but extraordinarily kind, helpful, and very hospitable. Returning the second time after being gone two years was almost like a homecoming to us Americans. Even one of my students from the first visit became my translator for the second visit! She was more than a hostess—more like a younger sister or a daughter. She also discovered the Lord on the first visit, so we felt closer, having that in common. The translator for the whole group each morning was a college professor from the University of Moscow. He wasn't merely a sentence-by-sentence translator but an instantaneous translator without hesitation. A really great thing was that he had connections from one of the former seminars months before. He needed this work to get some extra money, which was much needed for a college professor. He enjoyed this work, as he loved the Lord and certainly us Americans as well.

The outstanding thing about my first trip to Siberia was that I had an experienced sidekick—my well-traveled daughter Ilene. She had already led and directed groups like this to the area. Even though I had directed many tours, I needed a lot of help on this one.

The people there had their roots two or more generations back in the Caspian Sea area, where they were forcibly replaced by the Communist ranchers. After Communism was gone, they still felt, even after many decades, that this was their home. Not a word was heard about ever returning to the Caspian Sea.

The following article about our trip for the *North County Times* was written by Leslie Ridgeway.

OCEANSIDE PASTOR INSTRUCTS RUSSIAN TEACHERS

Concerns about young people seeing the world according to man and not God led the Rev. Orville Hiepler to Russia for a second time. Hiepler, pastor of the community Bible Church, a Lutheran Church in Oceanside, traveled to Tomsk, in the state of Siberia, for a little over a week in the mid-March. He went with Campus Crusade for Christ's international School Project, aims to help reduce moral decline in other countries, among other things.

Hiepler and thirty-five other representatives of Campus Crusade went to Russia to teach public schoolteachers and administrators morals and ethics from the Bible so that they could pass them on to students. That's a big contrast to the United

States, where religious doctrine is not taught in public schools, but Hiepler said "the Russian people need what the Bible offers."

"Many parents do recognize that something has to be done rather than build more jails. Something has to change inside youth to stop the slide into juvenile delinquency, gangs, and bad morals."

Some recent articles on crime in Russia indicate that crime indeed is up in some areas. One written by Peace Corps volunteer Time Goodwin said Russia had a murder rate of twenty-two people for every 100,000, more than twice the US rate. Though murders are on the rise, rape, assault causing bodily harm, and aggravated assault has leveled off, he said. "Another article indicated government officials were often the murder subjects."

Visited in 1959

This was Hiepler's second trip to Russia. He visited Moscow in 1959, when it was still the Soviet Union, on a tour of four communist countries. He said he noticed several significant differences in this trip.

"There was no restriction on cameras this time," he said "and there was no visible military presence. There was openness. In 1959, the fear of someone hearing a person talking to an American was constantly present."

On his first trip, Hiepler said he and his companions had to leave magazines and newspapers in restrooms or hotels where Soviet people could "accidentally" find them. His group was watched wherever they went, and their luggage was searched when they left their hotel rooms.

"We placed pieces of paper between items in our suitcases, and at the end of the day, the pieces had been moved," he said.

"Long lines for food and other essentials are gone, and free enterprise is in full swing, but not working well," he said.

"The sad part is, inflation has increased proportionately," Hiepler said. Hiepler and the Campus Crusade group went to Tomsk to meet with 500 public school teachers and administrators to teach them "how the Bible is reliable," he said. "We help them understand the Bible is God's inerrant word." They show this, Hiepler said, by using history (secular and biblical), archeology, the fulfillment of prophecy and by proving that the Bible answers humanity's greatest needs: "Why am I here, and where am I going," he said.

"The man-centers view doesn't answer these questions, but leaves us in limbo," Hiepler said. Campus Crusade was asked by officials in the Russians department of education to teach the teachers because of Campus Crusade's "Jesus film," Hiepler said.

The two-hour film tells the story of Jesus' life, and was made by Warner Brothers in America in 1979, he said. The film made it to Russia in 1990, and Hiepler said his son-in-law Robert Bradberry, who distributes the film for Campus Crusade, was asked by Russian education officials to make the film available to all of Russia's sixty-five thousand public schools. "He promised every school would get one, but asked, 'Would you also like us to teach the teachers how to use it?'" Hiepler said.

"Campus Crusade for Christ—originally started in the mid-1950s as a campus ministry—augments the teachings of churches throughout the world," Hiepler said. The organization has one hundred thousand missionaries worldwide.

Administrators and teachers were told they offer the film and accompanying curriculum to their schools as a choice, Hiepler said. The Russian department of education was asked not to force schools to use it, he said. When asked if Russian parents had commented on the curriculum, Hiepler said most of the teachers and administrators the group talked to were parents, and "they couldn't praise us enough."

Campus Crusade is working on a curriculum for American schools. The curriculum should be finished later this year, and will be offered to private and public schools. "The basis of the curriculum is to offer our administrators, teachers and children a choice," he said. "We want to present the two choices in an optional way—the 'God view' of the world, and the 'Man view' of the world. People should have an opportunity to make a choice."

Easter letter 1999 from Tomsk, Siberia, Russia

Dobryy Den, "Good Day" from the Land of the Survivors!

When traveling fifteen time zones from home you think often about those you love—your family and friends. So I decided this morning to write an early Easter letter to you.

I just came back to my room from filling my water bottles. Something like in Biblical Samaria except here we have a water purifier which does the job. We can't brush our teeth with faucet water. I must hurry as we are meeting several who are grandchildren of the many political persons who were forced to leave the Caspian Sea area and came here. Now this city has a population of 500,000, all living in apartments. The communists had a great plan to keep everyone equal by building these gray buildings.

I am ready to go to our leader's room before we go out to face the fierce below-zero weather. It's –5 today but it was much colder before. However, being dressed for the cold makes the difference. I am speaking as a resource person with my translator teachers and then at 6 pm we will visit our first flat. I have the hostess presents ready and children's gifts as well. I found out that one of our hostesses has a car, but it is really her husband's car, as she couldn't afford to have a car on a teacher's salary of $30.00 per month.

Someone asks how is it going? Are you tired? Endurance, agility and strength have been taxed by the lack of elevators. We go up and down to our rooms many times a day and at the beginning I had to lug my 70 pound bag up the stairs for 3 floors as bellhops are not available in our area of Russia.

1. Two flats—visiting and having Bible studies, three stories up a narrow stairway—no elevators.

2. At two schools and one university we got our workout, as the cloak rooms, where we deposited our pounds of overcoats and shoes, always seemed to be on the third or fourth floor. Our classrooms were located on the first floor so we got our exercise without the benefit of an elevator.

3. Last night was the test of tests: walking almost two miles (the interpreter and I both needed exercise) but we encountered ridges of icy snow as they rarely shovel snow and use no salt. We dodged between the cars and ran into a shop to warm up, as it was below zero and our glasses froze. My interpreter was like my daughter, Ilene, when she was here three years before with me, and we would lock arms and walk to keep each other upright. Arriving at the school to be met by the headmistress and other administrators at 6:30 p.m., I thought, "If they only knew how insignificant this guy from CA was they wouldn't have put on such a royal reception." They served jelly sandwiches and nice warm chocolate drinks made right there in Tomsk. We had an hour Bible study on "God's view rather than Man's View of the World," with these well-dressed, educated, and most friendly ladies eagerly devouring all we taught. On the way home we were given a lift in a teacher's car. Even though it took me a few minutes to get my long legs into their little car, it was a welcome ride back to my hotel in the even colder night.

The Great fulfillment of this tour is that many of these teachers will come to faith and will live in it. They plan to continue these Bible studies and perhaps start others. It will be fun to meet many new Russian Christians in heaven if not here on earth again. He is risen!

We will leave you with a Russian Farewell! Dobryy Den (good day).

"FALLBROOK IN FLAMES"

The headlines read "Over 200 homes burned, evacuate immediately!" and "Inferno merges toward the ocean—300,000 people evacuated," and "Fires force largest exodus in state history."

This was our city! We lived in a very comfortable and what we considered safe area near the middle of a golf course...but it was not safe now!

Within a short time, our community became as silent as a cemetery. The threat of embers was frightening, and the sun's radiance was dimmed by smoke as in a Midwest dirt storm during the drought years of the '30s. I had played golf earlier in the day, but we were commanded to stop and get out. Our entire Sycamore Ranch area was under a fire siege.

What a shock! Florence and I were to become temporary transients, exiles, and refugees between October 29 and November 2, 2007. My at-first stubborn and self-sufficient nature eventually softened to "maybe we'd better accept Eva's second invitation to come and stay with them overnight." These friends lived about ten miles down Highway 76, and this was the only road open and the only way out of the area.

Another shock hit my otherwise independent spirit that had me thinking, *No one can tell me what I can and can't do with my own house that I paid for!* The three policemen guarding our area gate said, as we were leaving, "You must know that you cannot come back to your house once you leave, and it will probably be several days until we can let you return."

When I phoned the second night from our daughter Ilene's house in Lake Forest, my answering service was filled with close to thirty calls. I was relieved to know our house was still standing. By the fourth day, we decided to try to return to our house, as we had run out of some medicines and just wanted to be back in our own home. Upon our return, all was in order in our house, but after settling in, I happened to look out the window to see our house was surrounded by seven Gestapo-type armed policemen. I yelled to them that we were OK. No one as yet had returned to the homes in this area, and these men thought we might be looters. We did explain and got an "OK, you can stay," and we were thankful to the Lord.

Transitory, temporary
In reflecting on these two words, they take on a new meaning, and I have more appreciation and thankfulness for the "sure hope of our eternal home."

The apostle Paul realized the uncertainty of the most stable entities in this life when he wrote 2 Corinthians 5:1: "For we know when this house we live in is taken down when we die, and leave these bodies, we will have wonderful new bodies in heaven, homes that will be ours forever, made for us by God himself, not by human hands."

Back to Our Roots

Small coal cookstove versus minus-thirty-degree cold blast
When visiting our home in Fallbrook, sisters, nieces, and nephews are aghast as they recall that their four-bedroom home out on the prairie was dependent upon this small cookstove (pictured) for half of its heat for a family of six children. This cookstove held only one-third of the needed fuel for the night.

They were also looking at flat irons that Mother Hiepler used for all of the weekly ironing. And the kerosene lamp they saw was the only means of light in the house for several years. The lamp had to be filled every evening and the wicks trimmed and the chimney washed in order for it to shed any light. All from the early 1900s.

My dad, Gust Hiepler, was in his rocking chair so often that everyone in the family can still visualize him sitting in the chair drinking a cup of coffee or sucking on a pipe while listening to the radio.

The picture shown, even though it was taken in 2001 at my house in Fallbrook, California, was at least thirty years after my father left for heaven.

The heating, lighting, and plumbing at the farm were changed in 1947, but for many years and a generation before when there was only coal and wood heat, everyone was still happy and satisfied. They had innovations and inventions, and they made do with what they had.

Ruth and I by the cookstove, irons, and lamp from the early 1900s.

Longest drive in the golf tournament

At the one-hundredth anniversary of Zion Lutheran Church, I was awarded a beautiful blanket that would look wonderful on anyone's couch, bed, or even wall. It included pictures and writing about Tioga's history in colorful, attractive embroidery.

We were attending the anniversary at Zion Lutheran in Tioga, North Dakota, Florence's home church. We had enjoyed seeing Florence's niece, sister, and husband and many friends from her church. It was a great celebration with Pastor Roger and Helene leading music and sharing a wonderful message with us all.

Saturday afternoon many of us enjoyed golf at the Tioga course. Prizes were to be awarded later in the day.

This course had sand greens and had actually been a cattle pasture north of town. In contrast to Los Angeles, where we'd have to wait to get on a golf course, here we could go out and start playing almost any day without a starting time. On an average day, there wasn't even a "starter" or someone to collect our fee. You would just place a five-dollar bill in an open box, and everyone was on the honor system. (I was used to paying four times more.) It all seemed to work rather well, plus my friend, Comart, had a gasoline-powered golf cart that I could use when visiting. I felt like a boy who loved chocolate and had just landed a job in a chocolate factory with full pay.

Getting back to the golf tournament, I couldn't imagine how I could get this blanket as the award for having the longest drive. I was puzzled because my golf game was only an eighteen handicap, and the drives were not the best part of my game. This was a mystery. The church was full of visitors from all over the country for this special celebration and anniversary, and the awards were being announced. I listened very attentively to who had won this or that, and then someone was nice enough to announce that, in Tioga for this tournament, they do things a little differently for the person with "the longest drive." It would be given "to Orville Hiepler, who had the longest drive by driving seventeen hundred miles from Fallbrook California to this event!"

The Unbelievable Miracle of Faith and Works—El Cajon, California

I was privileged to assist Pastor John Kent and his congregation as they faced what appeared to them to be impossible odds in trying to acquire property for their church. The congregation had enjoyed some steady growth over a period of ten years. They had been self-sufficient and had been paying all of their bills without any hiccups. However, they were stuck. They were stuck having to rent facilities in order to carry on worship services and ministry functions. It was a time when storefront property rents were on the increase. Because of this, the congregation was forced to move from one rental property to another—five address changes over the course of their ten-year history.

A fabulous place to thrive and grow

It was definitely time for them to purchase their own church home—a place to grow and thrive—but how? Rental prices were high indeed, but purchasing land or an existing suitable building seemed impossible. The congregation had been looking for years for something that might fit their needs, but it seemed always out of their reach financially. Finally, they did run into a great property in a neighborhood near where they had been renting. The property was just across the street from an elementary school. There were two homes and a large building that could be used for their worship services, and it also had excellent parking. Once again, however, the price seemed out of the question.

Es muss gehen!—Many said it couldn't be done

This congregation, in an entire decade, had raised a not-so-paltry sum of $89,000, and now they had a good property in sight with an impossibly high price tag of $1.3 million. They were hopeful, but they were certainly on their heels at the same time. Many were saying it could not be done. Even the pastor was skeptical and didn't wish to see the congregation move into something that might eventually put too much pressure on the members. He was quick to point out the lack of any "deep pockets" among the faithful who made up the church body.

It took a most cooperative pastor to make it go

I had enjoyed a long relationship with both this pastor and his congregation, and I believed that it was time for them to finally pull the trigger on a property purchase of this kind. I met with Pastor Kent and discussed how this could indeed be done. The plan was to have an informational dinner, giving the entire congregation an opportunity to see together what this property might provide for them. A presentation was developed with photographs of the property and its buildings, and descriptions were given about how the property would be used. At the end of the evening, we asked those who were gathered to make pledges. Two kinds of pledges came in—pledges of monthly giving for the purchase of the new property, and up-front pledges of one-time gifts for the congregation's building fund to make the necessary down payment. On a side note, the president of the congregation at the time was actually against the idea of purchasing this property. He was concerned that the financial pressure might be too much for the congregation to bear. He voted against the purchase; however, he and his wife also made a substantial monthly pledge.

A sight to behold

What a joy it was to see a congregation come together for something that seemed too big even in their own eyes. The folks gathered in that room that night raised enough in three-year pledges and one-time gifts to secure a loan, make a substantial down payment, and make their monthly payments with ease. Usually in these types of situations, you can only count on a certain percentage of pledges coming in; however, this congregation exceeded the norm. Where they did fall short, new members coming in made up for the shortfall with pledges of their own, and in each of these cases, it was without any prompting. The Lord Jesus Himself was working in the midst of this group, and it was evident to everyone involved in the whole process.

Everything's working most successfully

As of this writing, it has been only seven years since this congregation acquired their property, yet in that short span of time the members have retired the majority of their mortgage. Their monthly mortgage payment is lower than the rental payments they used to make for substandard facilities. In addition, each and every month, some of those very generous folks who pledged for only three years have continued their pledge, giving even to the present time. This is making possible extra payments toward the principal loan amount every month.

What a privilege it was to help a young, wary, and, at some points, doubting congregation see exactly what is possible when the Lord aims to continue building His church. Just imagine if this congregation had not stepped out in faith believing that the Lord would go with them where they might be now, and how many moves they would have had to make trying to flee from rising rental prices.

This congregation stepped up to the plate and expected a home run

Helping this congregation to see its potential is good not just for this local body; indeed, it is good for the entire church. As some of these parishioners make moves with job changes and such, they will take this giving spirit and can-do attitude with them into their new congregational families. When one congregation steps up and is willing to act in faith, it can aid others as well. In fact, as I write about this congregation's story, I hope it encourages you, the reader, by seeing that Christ Jesus is still building His church and that you too can count on Him to be with you when you endeavor to do the same.

I am thankful to my friend Pastor John Kent for writing most of this chapter for me.

Reformation Lutheran Church

CHAPTER 7

A DEVASTATING TIME

MERRY CHRISTMAS, 1992
This is a letter to our friends from myself and Florence in 1992.

Merry Christmas!
December 5, 1992

Our Christmas love reaches out and across the miles to you. We wish that we could shake your hand and hug you good and proper.

These last 80 days have been really something! Very few periods in our rather eventful lives have been as glorious, as praise-filled and as moved by God. Florence and I have toured abroad fourteen times. The excitement that we are having in our growing mission church in Oceanside…the people in our church are wonderful. We are blest. To see God's glorious grace active in the lives of seven family units (twenty people) joining our church next Sunday. There will be 7 baptisms and then confirmation and reaffirmation.

HEALING: Yes, the saving of souls is God's miracle of grace for us poor sinners. He has chosen to extend His grace to the miracle of healing for our precious Nelene. Her last biopsy indicated all the marrow tumors were gone. We trust and pray that this is a permanent re-mission. Seeing her receive the life-giving marrow transplant proce-dure and now witnessing her life back home with her family is God's miracle.

PRAYER SUPPORT: A part of the miracle is the prayer support from the East Coast to the blue Pacific, from the wheat lands of North Dakota to the mountains of California. It has been the Lord's gra-ciousness that we have experienced through you and the 2,000 others in the form of encouragement and financial help.

FINANCIAL HELP FOR TRANSPLANT: You who are read-ing this have been angels from God in your concerns. We don't know how to thank you enough! Without friends, families and churches, this would have been next to impossible.

YOUR PRAYERS: I can almost hear my friend Stoa praying as he's driving down those crowded freeways of Seattle, "God, you've got to heal Nelene. Her three-year-old, her ten- and eleven-year-olds, and her husband and all of us need her." He told me that he would also say to God, "You know how many she speaks to at church or in the Christian Business Women's Group…They all need her. You must heal her." That's from our friend, Norris Stoa.

CHURCHES: Nelene's and Jim's church, each of our children's churches and ours from Pasco, Sacramento, Hawthorne and Camarillo and Oceanside have been most generous. We thank you! We love you! Words are inadequate.

A CLOSE FAMILY: July 1991 brought our family even clos-er than usual. We've always been close and been drawn closer with Nelene's diagnosis. They have forgotten their own plans and devoted time to Nelene and Jim's well-being. Dorene and Curt have been back and forth many times from Minneapolis. Mark and Michelle have spent hours with Nelene and Jim at doctors or in the hospital on their way home. Mark has spent hours in litigation with Health Net, hop-ing to make this treatment available to hundreds critically ill and that do not have friends and family as devoted as Nelene's. Ilene and Bob have always been there in a moment's notice to assist with the girls, bringing meals, providing child care. Florence has experienced an even closer time with Jim and the girls, going at 7 a.m. Monday mornings to see the girls off to school and to spend the day with Jenna so Nelene could sleep-off the negative effects of the chemo treatments. Often she would be there to welcome home the girls and Jim from school with dinner on the table.

Jim's responsibility to the home, to the girls and to Nelene has been tremendous. We have prayed for him knowing what added responsibilities were his. Jim's parents have taken care of Jenna for many days at different intervals. Alta and Ed have been superb. My four sisters and families and Florence's family as well have been so supportive.

PRECIOUS HOURS: The hours that I have been privileged to be with Nelene in quiet talk going and coming from the Norris Cancer Clinic is a gift for me. Yes, talking, laughing, praying and often weeping.

One of her favorite comfort passages is Jer. 29:11. "I know the plans I have for you," says the Lord. "They are plans for good and not for evil, to give you a future and a hope." Once, while in a doctor's office, I asked her for a piece of paper. She took one off a small tablet on which I noticed about forty Bible verses. "What are these?" I asked. "They are my GOD PROMISES. I go over them often," she said. It was about a week later at the peak of bad news concerning her condition that she, Jim and I were on our way to Loma Linda to question a doctor as to the reality of the breast cancer cells now in the marrow of the bone. Was this serious? We wanted HOPE. I glanced in the backseat through my mirror so see what she was doing and she was pleasantly assimilating and soaking in GOD PROMISES in her tablet book.

ALL NORMAL: We invite you to pray for a permanent remission and to thank God for her healing. Her hair is coming back and she has gained the right amount of weight and her counts are all normal. The next biopsy will be in January.

We thank God again for His saving grace for our soul and His
healing grace for our bodies.

Sincerely in His Wonderful Grace, Orville and Florence
We had such hope!

ARTICLE ON MARK

My son, Mark, an attorney and brother of Nelene, fought an insurance
company for coverage for his sister's bone-marrow transplant. This article, from the *Camarillo Star-Free Press*, describes Mark's crusade to
obtain treatment for Nelene's cancer.

A Camarillo golden boy fights back

Melissa
Eastman

IF EVER THERE was a golden boy at
Camarillo High School, Mark Hiepler,
Class of '80, was it. Fair-haired and quick
to smile, Hiepler moved to Camarillo with
his mother, minister father and three sisters in 1978, a newcomer at an age when
newcomers are not given the warmest of
welcomes.

It didn't matter. Two years later he was
student body president, a starter on the
basketball and tennis teams, a member of
the Leo Club, and was voted Class King
and senior "Best All Around."

Mark was humble about his gifts. He
had a way of taking a compliment and
turning it around so it shone back on the
person giving it. Talking to him was like
basking in sunshine; everything was
bright and warm and easy, and you believed it would always be that way.

Always is a favorite word of high school
kids. Life has an unkind way of showing
adults always sometimes isn't.

A year ago, Mark's older sister, Nelene,
who had married and moved to Temecula,
discovered she had breast cancer. Mark,
who still lives in Camarillo, spent the better part of the year mired in an entirely
new feeling — helplessness — while
Nelene, mother of three young children,
had two full mastectomies and heavy
doses of chemotherapy. In December,
Mark's close-knit family learned the cancer had spread to Nelene's bones. The
doctors gave her 18 months to live.

THERE WAS STILL a chance, though.

Doctors at USC's Kenneth Norris Jr.
Comprehensive Cancer Center could perform a bone-marrow operation. The 45-
day procedure would give her a 50 to 60
percent chance of remission. Nelene applied to the center and three weeks ago
learned she was accepted.

Then an insurance company pulled the
rug out.

Health Net, the state's second-largest
health-maintenance organization, decided
it would not cover the transplant, which
they say is an "investigational" procedure
for Nelene's type of cancer.

Mark believes Health Net just doesn't
want to pay for the expensive treatment.

"Nelene's had no major illnesses ever.
And then, in her moment of need, the
insurance company just walks out," he
said. "It could happen to any of us."

NORRIS CENTER DOCTORS said
they'll begin the transplant procedure
without the insurance company's approval
if the family deposits $150,000 with the
center by next week. The total bill could
come to $300,000.

At last, there was a tangible goal. Mark
shrugged off his helplessness and started
putting his gifts to work. He mailed out
more than 1,500 letters to Camarillo-area
friends, relatives and acquaintances, including many at First Lutheran Church,
where his father had ministered until
1989. Similar efforts took place in Temecula and throughout the state.

Friday, Mark organized a protest rally
outside the Woodland Hills headquarters
of Health Net. An attorney, he also filed a
suit seeking a court declaration that the
transplant is generally recognized in the
medical profession, forcing Health Net to
pay. The Hieplers' story spread.

Five dollars here, 10 dollars there.
Money started to come in the mail. As of
Monday, two weeks into the effort, they'd
raised $145,000, just $5,000 short of the
goal. Contributions are being sent to the
Nelene Fox Trust Fund, 2048 Sierra Mesa
Drive, Camarillo 93010. It was an aston-
ishing accomplishment, the kind that
seemed to come so easily to Mark Hiepler, the A-student, class King, Best-All-
Around. Always.

Thanks to the kindness of friends and
strangers, it's likely his sister will get a
chance to fight her cancer with the very
best technology. Mark understands even
the best might not be enough.

*(Melissa Eastman is a columnist for the
Star-Free Press.)*

Shooting the Rapids and Riding the Waves at Age Seventy-Three

Our youngest daughter, Nelene, the mother of three young girls and the wife of an excellent English teacher, was diagnosed with breast cancer at the age of thirty-eight. The initial surgery and follow-up treatments had seemed to be effective, but the cancer returned. The fight began when Nelene needed a bone-marrow transplant, which originally was to be covered by insurance but then, after waiting six weeks, was denied. Through family, friends, churches, walk-a-thons, radio, and TV, $250,000 were raised in ten days for a successful bone-marrow transplant. Our son, Mark, and his wife, Michelle, were leaders in the forward vanguard marching in the fight to save Nelene's life.

Someday we'll know why

This fight included care for her three daughters—four-year-old Jenna and her two big sisters, Natalie, eight, and Nicole, ten—as well as her constant inspiration and helpful husband, Jim. Jim, a teacher in middle school, who was a counselor in his own right to his students, their families, and other teachers, felt devastated by the possibility of losing his young wife. Nelene, being a powerful force in her church community and for the Lord, was a friend to all she met. At this time she was on the speakers' board for Christian Business Women of California and traveled statewide as well as to nearby states to speak, even under the rigors of the marrow transplant. All of us had hoped and prayed this was God's avenue for a permanent miracle. However, His ways are not always ours. The sacrificial gift of God is the perfect gift. Through His Son Jesus Christ we can someday live forever in heaven, where there is no sickness. I know, someday, the Lord will tell us why He wanted Nelene in the glories of heaven at the young age of forty.

As a thank you to Mark and Michelle for the hours they gave as attorneys during the family trauma of Nelene's diagnosis and the fight to save her and then losing our daughter to breast cancer, Florence and I invited them on an Alaskan cruise in the summer of 1993. Included in this gift of a cruise was the agreement that they would ride the white-water rapids with us on a scary Alaskan river ride.

We thought that shooting these vicious rapids in Alaska would be enjoyable, but in reality, they looked horribly dangerous to us neophytes. After inquiring about the upcoming adventure and getting a little more background about it, however, our hearts were warmed to learn that our guide and seaman at the helm of our boat had done this more than one time! Riding the bumps, jumps, and drops of the rapids (and I'm not a swimmer) brought to my mind the past three years of loving, caring, and being with our youngest daughter as she struggled for her life, eventually succumbing. In real life, our family had been riding the rapids and waves of life.

We then turned to the beauty of nature and all of God's creation that surrounded us on this cruise, and we were reminded that this is just a foretaste of what God has prepared for us in heaven and of what Nelene is now experiencing.

A LETTER TO MY SON-IN-LAW

6/14/94

Dear Jim,

The Lord has just given me this verse as we enter North Dakota from Minnesota, "It is good to give thanks unto the Lord and sing praises unto His name." Ps. 92:1

I was just thinking about you, Jim and thought what a wonderful verse to share with Jim as he begins a whole new chapter in his life in about one and a half weeks. My last full day in North Dakota was spent with you fishing in the great Lake Sacajawea just three years ago. We did have good luck even with a cloud hanging over us wondering about the medical outcome from Nelene's tests. We are now in Valley City, North Dakota, staying at the state university for our church convention. Weather is great, no mosquitoes yet; they'll come! The girls arrived at Dorene's two days after we left. We'll miss them, so sorry, because we will be back in Minneapolis after they have gone home.

Florence and I want to assure you that we are happy with your marriage to Jeanette. We are pleased and feel the Lord's leading in the fact that the girls have had these months to get acquainted with her and have related to her so well. What a contrast to a situation where all of a sudden a dad would bring a stepmother into the family where the children didn't know her. The Lord's guidance seemed to provide Jeanette even from the day of Nelene's "going home to glory." The Lord had already provided her through the hospice ministry.

Florence and I have made this transition more easily these past two months, Florence a little slower than I, but she has to the best of her ability adjusted. I heard her telling one of our friends in Moorhead about Jeanette and your marriage. She was telling it with gratitude!

I can understand how her grieving and working through this, a mother's heart, would be harder than even you and I. After all, she carried Nelene next to her heart for 9 months and in her heart all 40 years of her life. I sensed Florence and Nelene's close mother/daughter relationship not only when she was ill and traveled with her in several speaking engagements but as she prayed for her well-being as a girl, as a student, as a teacher, a wife and mother of three daughters…I'm sure you can picture this relationship.

I too have enjoyed closeness with you Jim with our investments, counsel, travels and just being together. I am pleased that you are accepting Mark's good personal and professional advice as you move into a whole new life.

I will send another card and note to you and Jeanette together. We are sending a beautiful gift to you and Jeanette from all of us; Mark will bring it with him to the wedding. (Thursday morning). We will be with you, at least in prayer on your wedding day. It is now Thursday and I just finished talking to all three girls and they seem to be enjoying their Minnesota safari. Oh yes, as you know Jim, anytime the girls would like to come to our home or if you needed a place for them to stay when you are on your wedding trip, please feel free to call on us.

We love you, Orville

An Interview with Michelle

This interview about the scholarships Mark and Michelle have established and other aspects of their community involvement is from a Pepperdine University publication.

What made you come to Pepperdine for your law degree?
Both Mark and I attended Pepperdine School of Law because of its commitment to frame our legal education within a Christian contest.

Did you meet at Pepperdine?
Yes, we were introduced in 1988 by Dean Phillips who asked us both to share a word of thanks to the university board at the California Club for the law scholarships we each had received. Dean Phillips says that the boy-girl selection was a "strategic setup." Shortly after that speech, Chancellor Runnels called Mark into his office and nudged him to ask me out on a date. When Mark did, I (who was living with Norville and Helen Young) told the exciting news to Mrs. Young (former first lady of Pepperdine). Mrs. Young clapped her hands and said, "I've been praying you two would get married."

When did you initially set up the scholarship in memory of Mark's sister?
We set up our scholarship following the jury's landmark verdict in Fox v. Health Net.

Can you tell me about her?
Nelene Hiepler Fox was Mark's older sister. Mark was particularly close with her and lived with her while studying for the bar exam. The homecoming queen at California Lutheran University, Nelene was a funny and vivacious character who deeply loved the Lord and her family.

When you graduated Pepperdine, did you plan to be as involved in the Pepperdine community as you are?
Yes, even as first-year law students, we realized that we had been adopted into the Pepperdine School of Law family. We attended Bible studies in our professors' and the dean's homes and were personally encouraged by them in and out of the classroom. To this day we consider our Pepperdine professors and the dean to be some of our most trusted mentors in our lives.

I see your family gives back to the community in several ways; what other organizations is your family involved with?
We provide nursing and ministry scholarships at Point Loma University and are faithful friends of Oaks Christian School, where I serve on the board of directors. Mark is also an elected member of the Camarillo Health Care District. We have been involved at Good Shepherd Church in Camarillo and now with Calvary Community Church and help lead a small group Bible study.

How do you think this scholarship inspires students, or even your own children, and helps them grow?
Hopefully, the scholarship reminds recipients of the courage it took for Nelene to simultaneously battle both breast cancer and one of the nation's largest HMOs. It is a reminder of the sanctity of contract and the value of human life.

CHAPTER 8

TOURS

HOW MOMENTS OF REFRESHMENT TRIGGER HOURS OF PRODUCTION

On vacations I continue to like to be productive. For example, I directed sixteen international tours, including six to the Holy Land. The preparation time was filled with education, Bible study, meeting new people, and helping each other. The participants came to our home for pre- and post-tour gatherings. Everyone became acquainted with one another before the tour began. We invited as many people as possible who enjoyed Christian fellowship to join our tour. We tried to saturate our travel groups with great anticipation, educating them on the possible coming adventures and the feeling that you can be busy and vacation at the same time. That's what I always enjoyed.

Vacation, to me, is doing what I want to do and enjoying it
Directing tours with a Christian spirit meant that you were on call often twenty-four hours a day. When someone in our group needed help or something unusual happened to our itinerary, we were stuck because we had thirty-five or more individuals for whom we felt

responsible. You knew where the buck stopped. We developed close relationships with all of the tour members who may have been only church attendees or strangers or friends of friends at first, but after traveling, became close to Florence and me. Many would ask to be first on the list for the next trip. We had the same people sign up for trip after trip.

I was always more busy than anyone else, always "pulling things out of my hat," which might have been new to most of the travelers on our tours. They learned very early on the tour that having a schedule and having a good attitude helped everyone to have an enjoyable time. It means that we worked and played hard on the trip so that we could share it with our families, clubs, churches, and schools. Tour members were always eager to share their experiences when they got home. The geography, unique customs, and world history we learned on each trip provided an enriching experience for all. It wasn't unusual that a fellow tour member was on the trip to receive credits toward work, college, or graduate work.

Moments of refreshment on tours included experiencing and participating in church services. We might find one similar to one at home or one very unfamiliar. It was a learning process. While in Poland before 1990, when Communism dominated, we found only a Roman Catholic Church in which to worship one Sunday, and it was near our hotel. It turned out to be a long-remembered experience. We stood through the fifty-minute service with no place to kneel, no chairs or pews, and worshipped our Lord and Savior. We took in all of the similarities and differences.

Our group joined in the old European traditional order of service as much as we could, even though it was in another language. On many of our tours, we would make arrangements ahead of time with a church or a pastor and share in a service with them. Many times it was through an interpreter and became another unique experience. The Lord has told us that "where two or three are gathered in His name, He is there in the midst" (Matthew 18:20).

Deep Sleep

Home robbery in a strange new land

We were so excited to see Ilene, Bob, and baby Lisa upon our arrival in Harare.

After entering a different time zone, enduring a sixteen-hour flight, and having a late-night visit, we fell into a deep sleep our first night in Harare, Zimbabwe, Africa. We never heard the thieves enter the house.

Familiar with frequent robberies as he was, Bob had two locks on all the doors, inside and out. Once you got inside, you couldn't get out except by key.

Bob had recently bought the house and felt reasonably secure, as every window and every opening to the outside had better-than-average iron bars. Apparently, a vendor or some fix-it man had an assistant who grabbed the opportunity to bend enough heavy iron bars on one window to permit the two robbers to enter at about 2:30 a.m., only a couple hours after we all had gone to bed. They took Florence's travel bag from the foot of our bed and a large new blanket from the baby's bed, as well as all of Ilene's new window treatments. They used the curtains to carry away the loot collected from the house. This included most of the groceries and gift items that Florence and I had brought from the good old United States for our kids. Items from the freezer, such as roasts, steaks, and hamburger, were missing. They even liked the easy-to-open cans of yogurt and proceeded to eat them all, before leaving with three or four large bags of things all wrapped up in Ilene's new drapes, making it easier to carry through the windows. Their transportation was on foot. Even people who made their way in an honest fashion did not own cars.

If we had awakened and scared them, they would have had no way to get out of the house except through the small window with bent bars. If they were in another part of the house when we awakened, they very likely would have behaved like wild animals trapped in a corner. Who knows what they might have done!

The police came to the house at about 4:00 a.m. and awakened Bob and then all of us to tell us that we had been robbed. We never heard a thing—not a sound; we were completely unaware in our state of deep sleep.

The police had intercepted the robbers as they ran across a park. They had dropped the stolen items along the way, and the police found some of the items in one "bag" made from Ilene's drapes. They also found Florence's carry-on bag with Ilene and Bob's address, thus identifying the scene of the robbery. Florence's shoes were found outside, not far from the house the next morning, by Bob as he was on his way to Sunday school. Later, the final two bags of items were found in the park. Except for the snacks that the robbers lunched on after their raid, everything was found and returned to us.

The police weren't sure but felt there could have been as many as four people inside, all having come through the bent-bar window.

We praised God that we were so sleepy that nothing could awaken us. His promise was certainly felt by all of us, as scripture says, "His hand will watch over you" (Psalm 121:5).

A WALK WITH A REAL KING

I can't believe it—a boyhood dream comes true

If I had even thought of it, the most I could ever have expected was maybe to see him in a group of people.

It all started when my daughter, Ilene, and son-in-law, Bob, answered the call from God to be a part of the Agape Movement of Campus Crusade for Christ and to be involved in world missions. This was 1973. They had each had a successful year in their respective careers, for which they had been well prepared by their five-plus years of education. Ilene had found that teachers could not find jobs and so substituted for a full year before she got a full-time contract in a high school in Orange County. (Incidentally, her first principal would have been Clinton Thomas, a high-school friend of mine from Epping, North

Dakota.) However, she never had a chance to begin her second school year because they had to start training to go to the mission field with no salary and no promise of any financial help, only that which they would raise and obtain from churches and friends who would like to be a part of their prayer ministry team and financial team. Raising money was no great joy on the part of Ilene, but Bob knew he was answering God's call and did it as naturally as a fish goes for water. The fruits of their labors were bountiful during their fourteen years in Africa.

The Lord had laid it upon my heart that we should immediately help spread the message of the mission by directing a "happy-go-lucky" tour group to Africa after Ilene and Bob had settled in Swaziland, in southern Africa. Ilene was overjoyed to hear that Swaziland was a place where teachers were in short supply. Schoolchildren would come to school and wait all day for a teacher to come. Now she could use her teaching gifts.

The organizing of our tour group worked out successfully in 1975, the second year that they were in Swaziland. Bob and Ilene mentioned that we should plan the tour to arrive for King Sobhuza's seventy-fifth birthday celebration—a diamond jubilee!

Astonishing number of wives and children and the viewing of ten thousand troops

We did get to the celebration and had gathered in bleacher seats situated in a semicircle in the fairgrounds area. All the bleacher seats were filled, but the ushers were kind to all twenty of us foreigners and found an opening, seating us in a most prestigious area right next to a thirty-member press core from almost that many countries.

First came the king's children in four buses—all four hundred of them. Very soon after, his wives—one hundred in all—were brought into the arena in buses. The entire audience was excitedly waiting for the time when the king would personally walk and view all the troops lined up in a row waiting for him to give them personal attention. This seventy-five-year-old king was quite dapper, a small but agile man and had changed from Western clothing into his tribal garb for the celebration. He was the oldest ruling monarch at that time and had served in this position a long time.

As a leader of our tour group, I was out in front, adjacent to the press core, and we were so close together you could hardly see where one group started and the other stopped. I had a regular camera and a movie camera strapped around my neck plus the camera bag. From all appearances, you could not tell the difference between me and a member of the press core.

Guess who gets press privileges?
The celebration organizers were very partial to the press and planned to permit two or three of them at one time to walk with the king, covering each segment of his walk. As they were handing out the numbers determining what group would go first and who would follow, they also gave me a number, and I didn't refuse it; I actually made it convenient for them! Apparently, my cameras and bags had covered my badge. Our tour group members knew nothing about what was happening until, to their enjoyment and amazement, they saw in the very first group their tour leader walking next to the king, viewing the troops! The only frightening thing was that Ilene and Bob knew the rules and the security measures taken and thought I might be arrested. I hadn't a worry in the world. The full pleasure and enjoyment of walking with the king was the only thing on my mind. Sometimes, ignorance is bliss!

DINING WITH THE PRIME MINISTER
He was the brother of King Sobhuza, and our group was invited to visit with him and his family. He had only three wives and twelve children.

I credit these opportunities to Bob and Ilene, as they found it advantageous to get acquainted with the political leaders. Their ministry was to the nationals. Our tour group was in awe to be included in the invitation to the home of the prime minister and to meet his family. Many security measures were taken, but probably less than we have in the United States.

The wonderfully prepared chicken dinner and the great fellowship in this large home were enhanced by a little audio tape I had brought along with me. When I announced to the family and our group during our little program of singing and talking that I had a tape of Jubo's voice, the number-one wife said loudly, "You mean our son, Jubo, is in that little tape?" She then called to all of the children upstairs in their rooms to come down to hear their brother. (Remember, we didn't have cell phones and very rarely called long distance.)

Voices blended beautifully
Sometime before we'd left on this trip, Ilene and Bob told us about the son of the prime minister and that he was going to school in LA. We had met him a few times before we went on this tour. He was a Christian and loved to sing. He and Florence had voices that really blended well and had sung a few duets. He was perhaps only nineteen years of age and the oldest child in the family. Recorded on the tape were several duets that Florence and he had sung. Jubo also spoke to his mother and his sisters and brothers, addressing each one by his or her name. I have never seen a group of children more excited, thrilled, and pleased. As they left the room after thirty minutes, they were talking to each other excitedly. We could hear the name Jubo in almost every sentence coming out of their mouths. Their great excitement was, however, controlled by the very best manners and demeanor.

Seeing these children so elated over hearing their brother's voice was a memorable experience for me!

Hang On to Your Hats!

Around the world in thirty-one days!
The following prose, written by Sina Berg, was a treasured anniversary gift given to us in 1970, beautifully outlining our travels and experiences around the world.

Norway   In June we culminated our studies and our plans
And traveled with the Hieplers to exotic foreign
lands.
The country of my parents we visited once
more—
It stirred—enchanted—thrilled me as it had
done before.
The majesty and beauty of Norway's "Sognefjord"
And the grandeur of the mountains, no language
can record.

Germany   Oberammergau enthralled us with its quaint old-
fashioned charm;
Brigette, our German hostess, was loveable and
warm.
Tremendous the performance of the famous
Passion Play,
In scope and depth depicting the life, the Truth,
the Way,
From Adam's fall in Eden, to Christ's cross and
agony
To purchase our redemption for all eternity.

Israel   We eagerly awaited the highlight of our trip
The HOLY LAND where Jesus in close
companionship
Walked with His twelve disciples, performing
acts of love,
And revealing God the Father who sent Him
from above.
JERUSALEM, JUDEA! The city of our dreams,
The site of sacred history, where every pathway
teems

With memories of Jesus so touching and sublime,
We sense His hallowed presence over the wrecks of time.
A most exalted moment we shared at the Garden Tomb
In natures lovely setting where shrubs and flowers bloom,
Partaking the Lord's Supper in serenity and peace,
In this holy sanctuary among the sheltering trees.
We saw the field where angels told shepherds of His birth
And Bethlehem where Jesus as a baby came to earth.
We viewed the Dead Sea parchments, then on to Galilee.
A sacred hour of worship beside the quiet Sea!
Capernaum—Caesarea—in memory thrill us yet—
This mystic land of Jesus, we never shall forget.

India   Detoured to Bombay in India, we saw depressing scenes,
The cripples and the beggars, the cows so gaunt and lean;
Our cultured guide informed us these conditions soon would end.
We liked the Park and shopping with Pastor's Indian friend.

Nepal   In Kathmandu, the rickshaws were colorful and gay;
But the temples to the Buddha's often filled us with dismay.

East Pakistan   Reunion with the Ottesons! What joy it was to greet
These dedicated servants! A culinary treat

Was the Pakistani dinner, with curry, rice and soup.
The shops and the doll factory delighted our group.
"The Bleises got their visas," this was the news
we heard
The eve before departure as we met to share the
Word,
With many missionaries—a cherished time of
prayer
Committing one another to God's abundant care.

Thailand Bangkok was a revelation as we gaily sailed along
The people lived in houseboats or houses on the
Klong;
They washed the clothes and bathed, and cleaned
the foodstuffs, too,
In the murky river waters. They smiled, "How
do you do?"
Their colorful floating markets we happily recall,
The strange new vegetables and fruits for one
and all.
The elaborate woodcarvings of their temples left
us cold,
The statues that they worshipped were hideous
and bold.

Hong Kong The Crown-colony of Britain had a glamour all
its own:
Hong Kong upon the island, on the mainland is
Kowloon;
The tour into the mountains, the boat ride on
the Bay,
In the New Territories, folks living the old way.
The welcome by the Baumans and their hospitality.

The Lutheran World Federation helps every refugee.
The thriving shops and merchants enticed us all to
spend;
Embroidered goods and sweaters, jewelry, and gifts
to send.

Japan   Kyoto, and then Osaka, then Expo 'Seventy':
The nations all depicted their progress and history;
To see our own pavilion, we waited long in line.
A chairlift to the Playland—to a restaurant to dine
On famous sukiyaki—to a pleasant mountain lake.
A party for the Hieplers, but alas, no wedding cake.
In Tokyo, a sermon in Japanese was heard,
We sensed the Christian Spirit, and the oneness in
the Lord.

USA   Hawaii, the finale of this trip around the world
The USS Arizona with our own flag unfurled.
New insights and impressions of many ways of life
The hopes and aspirations, the poverty and strife
Of folks in other countries, we had gained along the
way;
The friendship of tour members, we had enjoyed
each day.
There are so many memories, much more that I
could tell,
But here my tale has ended and I shall say farewell.
To relatives and neighbors, to loved ones far and near,
May the grace of God enrich you and grant a blessed
year.

Sincerely,
Sina Berg

Sina Berg was a poet laureate in her own right, a widowed North Dakota farm wife turned California Christian and day-school teacher.

MOUNTAINS OF GRACE

Mary and Syd Mountain

Our tour group experienced an unusual day in Trondheim, Norway. We were all planning to leave for Oslo the following day, and then a couple of days later we would all be on our way home to California and other parts of the country.

Some of our tour group had been together before to the Holy Land and Oberammergau and now had spent three weeks together. We were as close as a family can be. Mary and Syd Mountain had been with us about two years before on a previous trip. The Mountains were known as the little stately English couple, always together wherever they went. They were members of our church, Trinity Lutheran, in Hawthorne. Mary was a nurse and was always very helpful if someone on the tour had a scratch or needed a Band-Aid or some medical assistance. Mary was ready to answer anyone's question in her articulate English accent. We loved to hear her talk, and her words were often made more meaningful with little deliberate gestures. She and her husband loved the Lord and the church and loved to travel with our Christian group. No one had to guess whether Mr. and Mrs. Mountain were enjoying themselves. Their big smiles and very positive actions always indicated they were having a wonderful trip and enjoying everything in their senior citizen maturity.

Up to this time in all of our tours, only once did a lady need to visit a doctor's office and then stay a couple of days in the hospital to rest while the tour continued on a rough safari in Africa. We returned after a couple of days to meet up with her after her hospital stay. The rest of the group was ready to go on safari again, as it had been so much fun.

Kings are crowned here

On this particular day, Mary and Syd Mountain had been seen walking together to the famous Nidaros Cathedral, which was built as a Roman Catholic church but had become a Lutheran church during the Reformation. King Olaf is buried there, and kings of Norway are crowned in that church in Trondheim, Norway. They had decided to do their own thing that day.

At dinner that evening, something was different—someone was missing. People asked, "Where are the Mountains?"

Possibly they had stopped someplace on their way back from the cathedral to have dinner. This was not an unusual occurrence, but usually someone in the group was made aware of an absence.

On our way back to our room after supper, I was ready to stop at their room to check on them, but another tour member had left a little earlier and came rushing back to find me and tell me the news.

As our tour people would often do, they would prepare the evening before for their early departure the next day. We were going on to Oslo. The Mountains had just begun to put their things together about half an hour before dinner. Syd had just leaned over to put some things into his suitcase, and as he leaned over, he fell to the floor. Mary, being an active nurse, readily went to his side and used all methods of resuscitation. Nothing seemed to help. Mary must have continued for quite a long time doing everything she knew to help her much-loved husband. But all was in vain. Syd had passed away.

Never to return

I went to the room to find out what was happening, and a doctor had been called to assist Mary. As soon as it seemed proper, I called our group of thirty-five tour members together to explain what had happened. We immediately had prayer for Mary, and needless to say, we were all stunned. I have never seen a group of people react with more empathy than our travel family did. All were very concerned about

Mary. What would she do? Do you travel home with a body? Should we all stay with her? Will there be a funeral for Syd? Will she want to join the group for the trip home? So many questions and concerns arose. This group, usually a very jovial and spirited group, had now turned to a sympathetic, concerned, and very sad tour group.

Each evening of our tour we would close with a devotional. This particular evening some people thought we should just stay in our rooms out of respect for Syd Mountain. Mary, with her unbelievable attitude, said that she wanted to come to a devotional, as she wanted to meet with the group. At that time she told the group, who were very emotional, that she and Syd had just talked about having been to the Holy Land and now the holy land of the Norwegians, namely Norway. She said that they'd had their fondest desires fulfilled on this trip, and that just that day, when they took their casual walk to the great Nidaros Cathedral of Norway, their desires and dreams were completed. She wanted to sing praise songs with the group that evening. She said that she didn't want anyone to feel sorry for her. After all, Syd was already in heaven. She went on to mention and assure us that no one should feel like they couldn't laugh and have fun as we usually did. I, too, assured the people that Mary wanted to stay with the group until we reached our country.

Decisions were made. I would stay with Mary, and Florence and the Norwegian guide would direct the sightseeing in Oslo; if there were any needs, Florence and the guide could help. Mary and I would join the group in Oslo the next day. Together, we would board the plane for home as scheduled.

There were three of us at the funeral the next day: the funeral director, Mary, and myself. In Norway at that time, and most everywhere, it was a requirement that the body be cremated and that a funeral service be held by an ordained pastor. I was prepared to do that. It was a short and honorable service. Afterward, Mary and I flew across Norway to Oslo just in time to walk into the dining room where all of our tour members were eating their last dinner in Norway. As Mary and I walked into the room, all of our people stood up and applauded Mary in honor of her husband and her great love for all of us and for the love she had for Syd. The following day, we all flew back to Los Angeles.

Service at our home church
Several in the group who were not from the LA area decided to extend their stay in order to attend the funeral service, which we would have in our church. Mary and Syd had no children, so the service was held the next day. We sang many praise songs to our Lord Jesus Christ. He has given us the sure hope of our salvation, whether we pass on at our home, in a hospital, or on a tour.

The Lord provided mountains of grace to our wonderful Mary Mountain in this time of tremendous loss. "My grace is sufficient for you; my strength made perfect in weakness. The power of Christ may rest upon me" (2 Corinthians 12:9).

THIS TRAIN IS GOING WHERE?
In July of 1990, we had a group of thirty-five people touring Europe by bus. We went to many fascinating countries including Italy, Switzerland, Austria, Liechtenstein, and Germany, and we were fortunate to experience many interesting tourist sites along the highways and byways. When our tour group got to Germany, the official sixteen-day tour ended, and approximately twenty members of the group returned to the United States. Fifteen of us continued our journey by train to beautiful Norway. This is where the real adventure began. Our train trip turned out to be one of the most unusual and challenging events that anyone could imagine!

Hamburg or Oslo?
Our train trip from Germany to Denmark was very nice and calm, and everyone was thoroughly enjoying the train. However, when we arrived in Copenhagen, the real fun began! Somehow, the individual

train coach that we were on was switched and connected to a different train that was going in the opposite direction from where we wanted to go. Unbeknownst to us, we were now headed for Hamburg instead of Norway! We found this out from the conductor, who advised us that we only had a few precious minutes to get off this train and back into the train station to get on the correct train going to Norway. This meant that we had to get all of our baggage and packages and everything else that we were carrying out of the coach car as fast as we possibly could. You can just imagine the panic that we all felt. We sure didn't want to end up in Hamburg!

Fortunately, we all were able to get everything off this particular train. We then literally ran to the ticket window in the depot, and a very nice man told us which train we should be taking to Norway. Unfortunately, we now had to travel through Sweden on a separate train, which meant that, since we were not staying on one train but boarding a separate one, we had to go through customs again and show our passports. One member of our tour group was from South Africa. She needed a visa to travel through Sweden, which she did not have, so when we had to show our passports to board this new train, we decided to put her in the middle of our group, and we all just waved our passports and quickly boarded the train. It worked beautifully, and she got onto the train with the rest of us without any problem from customs. We all breathed a sigh of relief once the train pulled out of the station. (This would never be possible in 2015.)

But our adventure didn't end there! We originally had booked sleeper compartments on the train; however, since we were now on a different train, we were in regular compartments and had to sleep on seat benches all night traveling across Sweden. Now, you would think that there would be a lot of complaining among the tour group, but I must honestly say that not a single complaint was heard. Now, that's saying a lot for a group of travelers.

As it turned out, we had a nice breakfast on the train consisting of coffee, rolls, and jam and butter and arrived in Oslo, Norway, none the worse for wear and with plenty of enthusiasm for a great tour of beautiful Norway!

A special thanks to Carronne Van Nyhuis for recalling and sharing these incidents.

UNBELIEVABLE RIDES IN SIX DIFFERENT COUNTRIES ON FOUR CONTINENTS

In my childhood on the North Dakota prairies, we would ride the yearling steers and milk cows around the straw stack near the barn where the cattle would nose and graze to find a few kernels of grain. This was also the bedding on which they slept and would provide a safe landing for us kids to fall on when we would get thrown off the animals.

The shortest-legged animal I've ever ridden didn't need to carry me very far, and I wasn't interested in riding very far! A 150-pound turtle was my mode of transportation in central Africa for five minutes.

The Siberian Russian Railroad was one of the very few means of transportation in that area of the world. I had at least thirty teachers in my two classes on my trips there.

Donkeys would transport us from the boats up to the level land of the town near the Aegean Sea. The picture shows you that Florence's donkey was a bit slower than mine. Donkeys, like other rides, came in various sizes, and everyone rode donkeys up the steep hills.

The camels at the Great Pyramids in Egypt were fascinating! I was very happy that we didn't have to ride more than a half mile. The camels as well as the drivers had their own ideas, and that was an experience all its own.

From the bubble tram over New Zealand, we saw some awesome sights!

LIFE SPARKLES WITH ADVENTURE

"Take delight in the Lord and He will give you the desires of your heart" (Psalm 37:4).

Florence and I have often reminded one another that in our sixty-nine years of following God's calling and doing service for Him, our "jobs and occupations" of serving and loving people in need have given us much delight and satisfaction. We sometimes say to each other that we surely don't deserve to have so much fun. It is like a continual vacation. A vacation has been rightly described as "doing just what you want to do and enjoying it."

Vacation time, what's that?

We look back at our vacations with gratitude, having come out of the Great Depression of the '30s when none of us talked about vacations but rather were thankful that we had a job. We would never say that we deserved a vacation or had one coming. We did not need to go somewhere and lie around, but we did what we could do, did things that we liked, and went where we could to help someone. By doing so, we helped ourselves in the process.

For most of the first eleven years in the ministry, we would go back to the farm in North Dakota and be with our families. We chose to go at harvest time, which made our parents very happy. I would jump up on the John Deere combine in the harvest field the first day home, weather permitting, and I would continue running it until the day before we were ready to pack up and get back to our loving parish. I know of no one that I'd sooner work with and enjoy his company more than my precious dad, who was always most generous to us. He would pay me for helping, and we would tuck it away for when we needed to buy a dependable car. Even though the days were long, from early morning until late at night—which I was acquainted with, from my work in the ministry—it was different and a change of pace, and we felt good about helping on the farm.

Work during vacation was enjoyable
I could not enjoy anything more than to serve as a chaplain at a mountain or an ocean summer resort for a week or more. We even had church services at the campgrounds on Catalina Island and Carpenteria and enjoyed being there for the day. We had a golfing vacation in Hawaii and had services at the resort. I would plan my vacation when I had opportunities to speak at Bible camps in Washington, California, and South Dakota.

The very obvious and blessed advantage was not only the opportunity to minister to others on vacation but also that the experiences benefited our children. We were able to have each of our children be with us on a tour. We were also privileged to have granddaughters join us for a Norway trip and a Germany trip. For our sixtieth anniversary, we invited our children and grandchildren to join us on a tour to New

Zealand and Australia. This tour had the most educated guides of any tour we'd led. What fun to share this time with our loved ones! Our kids now look back with gratitude for these memories. We have hundreds of treasured memories of experiences we shared as a family. We often say that the Lord was so good to give us these opportunities, to search for new adventures and experiences during our lives.

CHAPTER 9

FAMILY

WOMEN?

I lived with ten women. That would be a shock, even in our very liberal society, especially in contrast to the solid family and the marriage I have. You may understand my math when I tell you that I'm counting my mother, Anna, my five sisters, my own three daughters, and my wife of sixty-nine years, Florence. That adds up to ten women!

Oh yes, I also have eight wonderful granddaughters, all of whom came before our two wonderful grandsons—the last of the grandchildren born to Florence and me. Dorene's girls are Rachel and Amy; Ilene's daughters are Lisa and Kari; Nelene's daughters are Nicole, Natalie, and Jenna; and Mark's children are Sarah, Ryan, and Paul. We are privileged to have had a good start on great-grandchildren as well! At the present, the race between boys and girls is tied up at four and four. Dorene's daughter, Amy, has Kai and Leena Miriam. Dorene's daughter, Rachel, has William Curtis. Nelene's daughter, Nicole, has Gracie, Austin, and Maddie Mae. In August, we welcomed the arrival of Ilene's grandchild, Mikan James, born to her oldest daughter, Lisa. Little Emma Nelene, born in April 2015 to Natalie, gives us four girls and four boys. Family is a blessing!

WHAT'S IN A NAME? IS A NAME HELPFUL TO MAKE THE NBA?

Is it helpful if your parents are five foot eleven inches and six foot five inches in height?

Is it helpful if your parents were significant college players, even co-captains?

Is it helpful if your parents played basketball post-college?

Is it helpful if your parents were on semipro teams?

Is it helpful if your parents traveled playing basketball intercontinentally while spreading the Gospel?

Is it helpful if your grandparents built state-of-the-art gymnasiums as places to play and worship?

Is it helpful if your great-grandparents led cheers at parents' basketball games?

Is it helpful if your parents were the most enthusiastic basketball players of the United States and Australia?

If the answer is *yes* to all of these, my great-grandson can't miss—he has them all! His name is not Kobe Bryant, a great hero of all basketball players in the 2000s, but his last name *is* Bryant. His name is not

George Mikan, my dad's hero on the Minnesota Lakers team fifty years ago, but his name *is* Mikan James Bryant.

My only regret is that I may not be here to see him play twenty-two years from now.

Bob and Ilene Bradberry; Lisa, James, and Mikan James Bryant

At birth, Mikan joined six other Hiepler Hall of Fame stars. An additional star, Emma, joined Natalie's family in April. Our future NBA players are all of my great-grandchildren (parents included in pictures).

Rachel, Matt, and William Delaney

Amy, Samir, Kai, and
Leena Lakhani

Nicole, Rob, Gracie, Maddie
Mae, and Austin Cannaday

Natalie, David, and
Emma Skillings

West Point in One Day

Some people, including our former president Eisenhower, took the regular four years to go through college. Sixty years later, I was privileged to go through in one day because of my talented granddaughter Nicole.

If I hadn't become a grandparent, I would not have gone to see my granddaughter Nicole at Marist College, Poughkeepsie, New York, where she received a full scholarship and all expenses paid for her four years of undergraduate work. If I hadn't become a grandparent, Nicole and Natalie and Jenna would not have all become championship pitchers in girls' softball in both high school and college. If I hadn't been a grandfather—and yes, I acknowledge that her parents had something to do with it—I couldn't have followed Nicole from California to New York and then to West Point to see her pitch against the girls' softball team at the great military center of education for our army.

We toured the campus that day and enjoyed watching the game even though her team lost. It was always a thrill for us to watch Nicole pitch with such precision and focus. This was accomplished by hard work, practice, determination, and commitment, which many young people do not have today. Jim, her dad, was also a steady, constant coach and support for her in junior high and high school, enabling her to receive a scholarship to attend a Division 1 school. Seeing West Point and its buildings, chapel included, where so many military leaders had attended, was so much fun, and then to see Nicole doing a good job with her softball team was the best. Just being with our granddaughter was a treat in itself. This opportunity enabled me to go through West Point in a day.

Nicole has taught and coached at a New York college and Campbell University in North Carolina as well as at a high school and is now the children's and youth director in her church in North Carolina. Nicole has supplied me with a wonderful grandson-in-law and three great-grandchildren—all three of whom I have baptized over a period of four years. Being a grandfather of ten, I continually look forward to other great blessings and new everyday adventures.

Like Nicole, her two sisters and three cousins have added their additional grandsons-in-law plus an additional three great-grandchildren to the family. You can see why Florence's and my cups are running over with true family joy! Just keep it all coming—we love it! God is so good.

"Bless the Lord oh my soul and forget not all of his benefits" (Psalm 103:2).

"We are a chosen people, and royal priesthood, a holy nation, God's special possession" (1 Peter 2:9).

THIS WAS NOT IN OUR PLANS

A nephew's death causes an about-face
My cell phone wasn't usually on, as it was used only for emergencies, but this particular morning in the summer of 2004, I had it on. We were

on our way back to California from being in Wisconsin, Minnesota, and the Williston, North Dakota, area. We had spent the night in Medora, North Dakota, and were about 130 miles on our way when we received the call from Dorene that my oldest nephew, Glenn, had died. He lived in Williston and was my oldest sister Gertie's son. We had just left Williston after visiting with my two dear sisters and precious nieces, Gayle and Gloria, and nephew Glenn and his two sons. We had been eager to get back home to California after being gone almost six weeks. After we talked with Glenn's sisters and son Blaine, I was pleased to stay to minister to my oldest sister's children and to have the burial service for my nephew. Glenn had had several physical limitations for some time, and we had visited him a few days prior. We expected him to be with us for years.

A most unique hearse was used; his own new, beautiful, red four-door Ford pickup carried him to the cemetery. He was a car man, a mechanic like his dad, and especially loved Fords. In a humorous way, he had once said to his son, Blaine, "I would like a Ford product to carry me to the cemetery." His wish came true. His best friend and son was the driver, with the other son in the front seat and uncle (me) and grandson in the backseat. It was a privilege for me to take this last truck ride with Glenn.

This was a deeply moving, serious, and blessed last trip with our dear Glenn to lay him to rest near his parents and grandparents.

Airport happenings
The next two happy events happened about six hundred miles apart and fifteen hundred miles from my home in California. For me, who doesn't travel much anymore, this was extraordinary and exciting, especially because it involved close relatives at airports.

The first happened at the Minneapolis-St. Paul International terminal when my daughter Ilene and I were returning to California after a speaking engagement at our seminary and Bible college. We were delayed in leaving, so I went walking for a little exercise. As I returned to our gate, amid a waiting line of people, I saw Ilene with a familiar-featured person. As I came closer, I recognized my niece, Debbie Syverson Oseland, from Colorado, who is the daughter of my youngest sister Shirley. She and her husband Chris, had come to see a Vikings game. After the expected hugs and endearing greetings, we had a short visit with some picture taking as well.

The second happening was in August 2014 at the Williston airport. I was returning to California after my speaking engagement at the Upper Missouri Bible Camp near Williston. Dorene and Ilene were waiting for me to get my boarding pass when Dorene turned around in the rather small waiting area and recognized a gentleman who had just taken a seat behind us. It was Blaine, my great-nephew (grandson to sister Gertie), who lives in the Phoenix, Arizona, area but has businesses in Williston. He was on his way to Minneapolis to meet up with his son, who was checking on a school interested in his hockey playing. Blaine is the son of my nephew Glenn. Glenn and Blaine were close buddies. They worked together, shared many interests, and had a very close father-son relationship. What fun it was to have a few minutes to share about the weekend and tell him that his Aunt Gloria, Aunt Gayle, and Arlan were at the Bible camp services and dedication of the Hiepler Lodge.

EXTRAORDINARY AND UNBELIEVABLE

Doctor of jurisprudence makes hospital calls
If a medical doctor made a house call in this day and age, that would make the news. It's also news when a doctor of jurisprudence and nationally known trial lawyer visits a church friend or casual acquaintance in a hospital or at his home, or a ninety-four-year-old friend he casually met while visiting his mother at her care center. When you realize these visits are not with clients or prospective customers, this is really news. It is also the sign of a caring and loving human being.

His staff of several lawyers and support staff know him as the one who will drop everything in his busy practice to help out a person in need. His sister's case in 1993 was great evidence of the love he has for family.

When his family reminds him of being elected student body president of his Camarillo high school, after having been there only a little over a year, and the same year being elected homecoming king, he just turns his head and pays no attention. Oh yes, he also was selected to speak with the governor of California at his law school graduation. That is extraordinary. I have a picture of a plaque with his name among the Top 100 Most Influential Lawyers in the America, by the *National Law Review*. I'm sure you have figured out by now that I am speaking of our son, Mark. I am a very proud father.

His local honors are especially important and point out his benevolent spirit in his home city. He serves on the board and is vice president of the Camarillo Health Board. He received the Ventura County Bar Association's Public Service Award (Ben Nordman Public Service Award) for volunteer work and philanthropy. As a very attentive family man with a wife of twenty-three years, he takes an active role in his two high-school children's and college daughter's lives.

I have been the recipient of his consideration and helpfulness even in his super busy schedule. He arranged depositions and appointments in Minneapolis at the time I was speaking at the AFLC (Association of Free Lutheran Congregations) seminary and Bible school and showed up in the audience—a real surprise for me! Another time four years ago, he made arrangements so that he could work out of San Diego the seven days I was in the hospital and was always there for me. This doctor of jurisprudence makes hospital calls as well as home visits, and I thank God daily for my wonderful, extraordinary son.

FAMILY PHOTOS COLLAGE

CHAPTER 10

How I See It—Lessons Learned

A Stranger Moved In

The following is from the website of Fr. Tommy Lane SSL, STD.

From the beginning, Dad was fascinated with this enchanting newcomer and soon invited him to live with our family. The stranger was quick to accept and was around to welcome me into the world a few months later. As I grew up, I never questioned his place in our family.

Mom taught me to love the word of God, and Dad taught me to obey it. But the stranger was our storyteller. He could weave the most fascinating tales. Adventures, mysteries, and comedies were daily conversations. Our whole family was held spellbound for hours each evening.

He was like a friend to the whole family. He took Dad, Bill, and me to our first major league baseball games. He was always encouraging us to see the movies, and he even made arrangements to introduce us to several movie stars.

Dad didn't seem to mind, but sometimes Mom would quietly get up (while the rest of us were enthralled with one of his stories of faraway places) and go to her room [to] read her Bible and pray. I wonder now if she ever prayed that the stranger would leave.

You see my dad ruled the house with certain moral convictions, but this stranger never felt an obligation to honor them. Profanity, for example, was not allowed in our house, not from us, from our friends or adults. Our long time visitor, however, used occasional four letter words that burned my ears and made Dad squirm. To my knowledge, the stranger was never confronted. My dad was a teetotaler who didn't permit alcohol in his home, not even for cooking, but the stranger felt we needed exposure and enlightened us to other ways of life. He offered us beer and other alcoholic beverages often. He made cigarettes look tasty, cigars manly, and pipes distinguished. He talked freely (much too freely) about sex. His comments were sometimes blatant, sometimes suggestive and generally embarrassing. I know now that my early concepts of the Man/Woman relationship were influenced by the stranger.

As I look back, I believe it was by the grace of God that the stranger did not influence us more.

Time after time he opposed the values of my parents, yet he was seldom rebuked and never asked to leave. Many years have passed since the stranger moved in with this young family on Morningside Drive. If I were to walk into my parents' den today, I would still see him sitting over in a corner, waiting for someone to listen to him talk and watch him draw his pictures. His name? We always called him TV.

As I recall, this letter came to me a few years ago. I was asked to read it and pass it on. I sent it out in a Christmas letter a couple of years ago.

Attracting New People

New people, new growth, and new buildings catch everyone's favorable attention. People like to be in a community where there is excitement and progress. This has a perpetual effect: success breeds success.

The opposite is also true: failure breeds failure.

What new family visiting your place of business, your school, or your church checks to see what you have to offer and is greatly influenced by that first visit? If there is excitement and interest, there is likely to be a second visit with more questions.

If I were looking for a church and every three months I noticed a group of people were new members to the congregation, I would be greatly impressed and wonder why there was such interest in this church. I would see progress, not stagnation, or the "same old same old."

Of great importance would be a friendly and welcoming the pastor, greeting people at the door. My first impression would then be, "Wow, they really care about me." Perhaps the pastor even asks if he could be of help in any way, tells me he would remember me in prayer, and says he hopes to see me back the next Sunday in church. The pastor or greeter could also get my name and address by having me sign a guest book and then have a follow-up call the next day or so and invite me back the following Sunday. If I received this treatment, I would have a warm feeling about this church community.

Eight building programs and church growth proved this to me through the years.

It is sometimes felt that we have to take away valuable time from Bible studies and evangelism to prepare and do a church-building program. That is somewhat true, and it also makes everyone work more diligently together, but we can do it all. Everyone needs to be motivated and at top-notch speed doing the Lord's work in the most effective way with enthusiasm.

This is also true: enthusiasm breeds enthusiasm, and indifference breeds indifference.

Es muss gehen! (It must go!)

Church attendance doubles

It has happened more than once in new churches and in older, complacent ones that when they reach a time when expansion is needed, new enthusiasm, new people, and new accomplishments happen. The expansion does not stop at the day of dedicating new facilities but carries over into the future, and many more souls are reached for heaven and His Kingdom. Actually moving into a new facility can bring in twice as many people as when they started the project. With God as our focus, we should expect much good fruit.

God's Word promises that "I am the vine, you are the branches. If you remain in me and I in you, you bear much fruit, for without me, you can do nothing" (John 15:5).

"Refirement" starts at retirement sometimes

I don't take the credit but would like to share with you how the Lord has given us the opportunities for expansion and the willingness to see them through. It started with the fun and satisfaction of starting new congregations. When I see to this day a new area where new homes are being built and people are moving in, I feel like a farmer with a bumper crop waiting to be harvested.

Even today, I hear families and parents tell me that they would not be on the road to heaven and in a good church if it had not been for the new church that started in their area and for the fact that I lovingly invited them to join me at that new church.

Rewards come unexpectedly

Yesterday Danny Moss, from West Sacramento, called me. I hadn't talked to him since 1959 when he was a good-looking twelve-year-old freckle-faced boy in our Sunday school and day school. He used that description of himself being "a freckle-faced boy," thinking I wouldn't remember him. Not only did I remember him, but I recalled how his whole family was living in the area where I went door to door sharing the Good News and inviting them to church. What a joy to talk about

Gloria Dei and the wonderful events we had shared at that church. I had invited his family to our church, which hadn't even started yet, but I was planning at that time to temporarily meet in a mausoleum chapel in the cemetery in Sacramento. Moss family members were leaders in our church and in our school.

You'll never forget
The following is an excerpt from the book *Out of the Salt Shaker and into the World*, by Rebecca Manley Pippert.

His name was John. He had wild hair and wore a T-shirt with holes in it, jeans, and no shoes. This was literally his wardrobe for his entire four years of college. He was brilliant. Kind of esoteric and very, very bright. He became a Christian while attending college.

Across the street from the campus was a well-dressed, very conservative church. They wanted to develop a ministry to the students but were not sure how to go about it.

One day, John decided to go there. He walked in with no shoes, jeans, T-shirt, and wild hair. The sermon had already started, so John started down the aisle looking for a seat. The church was completely packed, and he couldn't find a seat. The people were beginning to look a bit uncomfortable, but no one said anything. John got closer and closer to the pulpit. When he realized there were no seats, he just squatted down right on the carpet. (Although perfectly acceptable behavior at a college fellowship, trust me, this had never happened in this church before!) By now the people were really uptight, and the tension in the air was thick.

About this time the minister realized that a deacon was slowly making his way toward John from the back of the church. The deacon, in his eighties, had silver-gray hair, a three-piece suit, and a pocket watch. A godly man, he was very elegant, very dignified and very courtly. He walked with a cane and as he started walking toward this boy, everyone was thinking, *You can't blame him for what he's going to do. How can you expect a man of his age and of his background to understand some college kid on the floor?*

It took a long time for the man to reach the boy; the church was utterly silent except for the clicking of the man's cane. All eyes were focused on him. The minister couldn't even preach the sermon until the deacon did what he had to do. They then saw this elderly man drop his cane on the floor. With great difficulty, he lowered himself and sat next to John to worship with him so he wouldn't be alone. Everyone choked up with emotion. When the minister gained control, he said, "What I'm about to preach, you'll never remember. What you have just seen, you will never forget."

MAXIMIZING THE VALUE OF WORSHIP LITURGY

Why this is so meaningful to me
At times it may seem to be only words; however, those words may have power in themselves. These words, with many variations through years, have helped form our Sunday morning liturgy and worship. The history of this came out of the American Lutherans accepting the efforts of Henry Melchior Muhlenberg, a German, in laying a foundation in 1748 for common Christian liturgy in America. Further effort resulted in the Common Service Book (1917). This coincided with the merger of several Lutheran bodies in 1917.

I was inspired by the worship in larger churches during my college years. The liturgy included the Lord's Prayer, the Apostle's Creed, and the Athanasian Creed, as well as opening and closing prayers and benediction. These all have stood the test of time. To me, nothing could be more meaningful and impressive than the Gloria, the Kyrie, and the Agnus Dei when sung from the heart.

This chapter isn't intended to be a directive in your worship but rather an expression of thanks for the churches that want to use these great expressions of our faith Sunday after Sunday. These are proven over time and come right from the Word of God and so are superior to anything I might formulate to make worship more meaningful.

Over these seventy years in the Gospel ministry, I have noticed in times of illness, old age, and death, people repeating and clinging to the Word of God as expressed in these liturgies, creeds, and prayers. I find myself relying regularly in a prayer that my confirmation pastor said we should pray daily—the perfect prayer: the Lord's Prayer. It is all inclusive and enables us to pray for so many important needs in just a few words. I pray it over and over again when facing surgery, important treatments, or when I am feeling a great need to be closer to God. I have also recited these gifts of liturgy with those nearing the end of life. These come back into the mind and many recite or pray the familiar as they grow close to heaven. Florence and I together daily recite the Lord's Prayer, say memorized evening prayers as we taught our children, and also sing familiar hymns together.

Hymns endure

I believe the tried-and-true hymns over the ages should continue to be a part of our worship. Memorizing them as we had many years before has given me more to base my faith upon, as these hymns express and put God's Word into music as the Psalmists had already done as revealed in the book of Psalms.

In our daily and corporate worship, there is a place for contemporary worship songs that glorify the name of Jesus. Many churches have found that blended worship works well for them, especially when coming from the strict liturgical background of our Lutheran churches. If we are to open our church fellowship to those who may not come from the same background as we have, we need to offer choices in worship or be flexible and blend our practices of liturgy and worship.

Six Statements That Impacted My Life

1. "All things are possible for the Lord."
2. People would ask in German, "*Wie geht's?*" Translated, that is "How are things going today?" My dad would answer, *Es muss gehen!* or "It must go!"
3. My grade-school teacher, Mrs. Sanderson, would always say, "*Can't* died; *can* is alive."
4. My drama and speech coach in college, Mrs. Osby, who was a short, stout, dynamic woman, would get on top of a low table and stamp her feet loudly to get our attention. She would almost yell and say, "You are afraid? You are scared of *what*? 'God did not give you the spirit of fear, but of power, love, and a sound mind.' Use it! Use it! Now go over the words again, and do it as though you are God's son or daughter and not based in fear."
5. "Tithing is a privilege." As a freshman in college, I was influenced by two of my senior college friends, Orvis Hanson and Torval Torvik, who were leaders on campus and who both loved the Lord so much that they spoke of giving a tithe and practiced it. They gave from meager salaries, many as small as my seventeen cents an hour up to thirty cents an hour, and spoke of giving their tithes as a privilege, almost like I would speak of winning a game of checkers or horseshoes. I said to myself, *If they can do it and be so happy, I will do it also.* Even during our country's worst Depression, with nine out of ten years in the '30s experiencing crop failure, my parents still went to church and gave to their church.
6. Maybe the crowning event came in 1943, during my second year in seminary, when I heard the great manufacturer of earth-moving machinery, Robert LeTourneau, speak in Minneapolis to a youth convention. He said that less than ten years before he was $200,000 in debt (which is equivalent to $4 million today), and this was in the middle of the Great Depression; however,

God touched him, and he gave his heart to the Lord. He began tithing out of thanksgiving for the little he did have and with the belief that "God loves a cheerful giver," which led to his success. He had become able to tithe 90 percent and keep 10 percent. He urged us to do the same. He was a very unassuming person, looking much like a poor working farmer, and spoke about success and giving back joyfully in thankfulness for all God had given him. God increased his business, so he paid off his debt and used the inventive mind that God had given him. I recall seeing a tractor at a road-construction site with the LeTourneau name on it. That was amazing! This wealthy person really piqued my interest at this time. We had only spoken of two well-known millionaires previously: namely, Henry Ford and John D. Rockefeller. Another time, I recall standing on a street in Minneapolis when a passerby gave me a Gospel tract from the LeTourneau Publishing Company. Only recently, my friend, Ron Spooner from Camarillo, sent his son to the LeTourneau University in Texas. Think of the many people this man has influenced through the ways he has shared his wealth! I heard him speak at my Rotary club in Hawthorne. He accomplished his goal of giving 90 percent of his income to the Lord and living on 10 percent. The 10 percent had become much larger than the 90 percent when he'd begun tithing some years before.

God and family—which comes first?
The entire ministry of giving is tied into always remembering the two most important entities: God and family. Some have felt that the Bible could be understood to mean that the family is first when the income is low. My experience has been the other way. When we honor God in the tough times first, your family will receive even more. My first salary of $1800 a year in 1945 was one of the lowest salaries. I began immediately tithing with my first salary; Florence and I have always put our

tithe aside first, and we have been abundantly blessed. Yes, all things are possible for the Lord.

UNIQUE ADVERTISING

"You can delegate authority but you cannot delegate responsibility."

I like the above quote by Byron Dorgan as well as the one I saw recently in the newspaper: "Like all successful organizations, it takes special people at the top to set goals and then design strategies to meet them." This emphasis is very vital in the realm of business, politics, and even in the ministry.

I had the privilege of meeting Woody Knight, the governor of California, in the 1950s. He was a man who put the above quotation into action, even helping us in our Simultaneous Evangelism Emphasis (SEE). I was privileged to be chairman of the publicity committee during this week of meetings, and Governor Knight welcomed Pastor Lundgren and me into his office. I pinned a SEE pin on him, and he encouraged our endeavors throughout the city. The good will of the governor and the many businessmen in our church caused the SEE to be a great success throughout the city and for our church. As Jeremiah 20:20 says, "Call to me and I will answer you and I will show you great and mighty things that you do not know." Isn't it wonderful for you and for me when we know our present and our future are totally in His hands?

Searchlight

For three hours, a large antiaircraft searchlight could be seen throughout the sky over Sacramento. This was the first night of our Preaching, Teaching, Reaching mission. Everyone in the capital city could see this ray of light, and people across the city were inquiring, "What is going on in South Sacramento? A new business? A carnival?"

The cost of rental and of manning the light for four hours each night was minimal compared to the publicity a newspaper gave us. The results of reaching out to people who attended our meetings were significant. People just followed the light! We followed up with these new people and welcomed them to our community.

The pictures appeared in the *Sacramento Bee* newspaper.

UNBELIEVABLE CHANGES IN PROPERTY VALUES

The cost of a parsonage jumped from $11,000 to $873,000 in sixty-five years. Incomprehensible in 1945!

After we were married, Florence and I lived in the small church basement and later moved a couple of times to different homes of parishioners. Finally, we moved into the first major purchase of the congregation, a beautiful house across the street from the church. The cost? Eleven thousand dollars. This was quite an upscale house that had been owned by a realtor. It had a beautiful fireplace, separate garage, beautiful built-in china cabinets in the dining area, and a well-lit kitchen with pantry and first floor and basement bedrooms. The basement was set up as a very nice apartment, which we immediately rented out at twenty-five dollars a month. It helped the congregation make the payments on this large purchase.

The first bedroom off from the front porch and main entrance to the house served as the church office. Since there were two bedrooms on the main floor, we took the back bedroom, which had full ceiling-to-floor windows. Quite an awesome room! As each of the three girls were born during our seven years in Pasco, all of them plus a bassinet, crib, and single bed found a cozy life in the back bedroom of the house. The office was also used as a guest bedroom when our parents came to visit (at one time for two weeks and up to three months at another time). The downstairs was rented by a public school teacher and her husband.

After about five years, the basement was changed from a rental, the church loan was paid down, and our house was used for an overflowing Sunday school as well as evening meetings and church gatherings, especially during the building of the new church in 1950. Our house would be called a parish hall in this day and age. The proximity of the house to the church was a great advantage for the growing church.

A house on wheels—moving to a new address

In Hawthorne, the parsonage was next door to the school and across the street from the church.

People from the congregation on Sundays would walk in and make a cup of coffee or come in and visit with friends in our living room. We were not used to this, and it was a good way to get to know people a little better. The church and school had some major growth spurts, so it was decided that we would buy our own home. This was advantageous for a pastor, as he would then have an investment, and the church could use the cost of owning a house some other way. This house (a parsonage as the pastor's house was called) would be taken down or moved to another property. It was at a time when the Interstate 405 was being built, and many homes were being moved from the swath that the freeway would make through Hawthorne. Houses were plentiful and available to purchase rather inexpensively if you had a lot onto which to move them. We in turn loved this house and the guesthouse in the back, so we decided that if the church wanted to sell us the house, we would find a lot and move the parsonage. They wanted to give it to us just to get rid of it, as the new educational building was being planned for the property. We were so thankful and gave the church a thousand dollars. We would own our own house, which would help us in future investing, and we purchased the only lot around that was sixty-plus-feet wide, which was needed for our house. An old, dilapidated house on the property was torn down, and we found a company to move the house the mile and a half.

Nighttime move

The day—or night, I should say—of the move arrived. It was less disturbing to the community and traffic if done during the night. The interior only needed breakable things taken off the walls and pictures placed on the floor. Otherwise, everything was left just as it was. The move began. The house was on a small hill and had to be moved down over a curb and onto the street. A man rode on top, and as he came to telephone wires or power lines he would cut them, enabling the house to go through, and then splice the wires back together. A real task and a well-engineered event took place in Hawthorne that August night of 1963. Florence and the younger children had gone to North Dakota during this transition.

Emergency room visit, 2:00 a.m.

Dorene and I set the alarm for 2:00 a.m. to watch this move take place.

Ditches were dug; electrical and plumbing were all in the ground and ready for the house to be placed on top. This was California, so there were no basements to deal with. I had made up the blueprints to combine the guesthouse with the main house on the new property. As we walked around the property, checking where the various rooms would be placed, Dorene let out a yell! A steel reinforcement piece had found her foot. In the darkness, it was difficult to see the extent of the injury, but I could tell she was in pain. We immediately headed to the emergency room where Dorene received eight stitches and was told not to walk on the foot for three weeks. The move was a success, however, and the house became a fixture on a perfect-sized lot on Washington Avenue. This was our home for the next fourteen years.

Our lot cost $6,500, and with the move and rebuilding and compilation of the three buildings, the total cost was $40,000. The cost of this house was minimal in comparison to others around, but it was ours! We sold it for $85,000 in 1978 and bought a new home in Camarillo for $92,000 with a view lot. In 1990, we sold our Camarillo house for $322,000. You know how this works. Then we needed a house in Fallbrook.

Dream home

Born in a small three-room house with two rooms attached to a homestead shack, I couldn't believe that at age seventy I would be able to help design and have my good friend Noell Hand build our beautiful house. This house was situated above the eighth hole at the Fallbrook Golf Club. Fallbrook, being the avocado capital, was laden with avocado groves as well as orange trees and various citrus. Sometimes we'd have a view of the Palomar Mountains to the east. I planted many fruit trees on the side of the hill, which made me think back on my farming roots in North Dakota. This area had a very rural feeling, yet it was quite populated. We were in the process of starting congregations and felt this was a good central area for us in this North San Diego County.

Chuck Bennett, a college friend from Jamestown, North Dakota, and a minister on the East Coast for many years, said to me once, "I hesitate to become too attached to my home on earth in case I may think less of my heavenly home." This was a beautiful place, and we loved it. After twelve years, we decided that we needed a one-level home, but we didn't want to leave the area. After a sale, we downsized a bit to Sycamore Ranch just down the road a mile. It is located on the country club golf course the Golf Club of California. It was a beautiful home where we lived until our return to Camarillo.

We continue renting out this house and have been able to borrow on it to help subsidize church buildings and parsonages and give any profit from its sales for scholarships to train students in seminary to be pastors.

Real estate fifty years later

In Camarillo, fifty years later, the parsonage was bought for $873,000. Through the bountiful goodness of our Lord giving us some extra cash, we purchased this house for the new pastor and family, and they have rented it from us. This was purchased at the time when real estate was a great investment. Due to the downturn in the real-estate market, we have lost money on this house and have it up for sale in 2015.

We experienced that this time of buying was similar to the time of buying in Pasco. Both houses were purchased at the peak of costs, with inflated prices. In Pasco, it was the discovery of the atomic bomb manufactured in nearby Richland, Washington, and in California, it was the boom right before the recession in house building. The similarities continue inasmuch as both were bought in the more desirable parts of town and both would be OK for resale.

The Lord is good. He has more than taken care of us and our family. We continue to work and pray as the Psalmist did when he played instruments and sang, "May God be gracious to us and bless us and make His face to shine upon us and give us peace so that His ways may be known on earth and His salvation among all nations" (Psalms 67:1).

Six major building projects

The following was written by my daughter, Dorene.

Amazing is the only word I have for directing and inspiring people in six congregations to see the need for these projects. Many call my dad "a visionary." He can see the big picture before many of us even have a thought in that direction. People were coming to find out who Jesus was through the various ministries, and my dad in turn could see the need for better and bigger facilities. A project could take anywhere from twelve to twenty-four months to plan and draw up, to find architects, and then to present a stewardship plan of funding and proper use of loans, which even included preparing the selling of bonds for the project. He hesitates to share these things because at the time it wasn't any big deal to him. He just saw a need and acted on it. To him it was just part of being a leader and shepherd of a congregation and of a school. It was a by-product of saving souls. Martin Luther was a great example of "championing Christian education" in every way possible, especially through Sunday school, elementary schools, confirmation, and adult Bible classes. My dad would often say, "What else can I do for the Lord?" It reminds me of the words of Isaac Watts: "Love so amazing, love so divine, demands my soul, my life, my all."

Properties purchased

Eighteen properties in various suburbs and cities where we lived were purchased during my dad's tenure. Some were difficult to come by. In Hawthorne, eleven properties were adjacent to the church. Building on these gave the Sunday school, day school, youth programs, and preschool room to expand. Two houses were connected to provide for the preschool. This building was enlarged again, and another two houses were included, surrounded by a beautiful preschool playground facility.

Youth a constant consideration in expansion

Four years after our coming to Hawthorne, a two-story classroom building was built, which housed a youth room, administration offices, library, and classrooms. Trinity was thinking of the young families as well when a very modern nursery facility was made available for infants to be cared for while their parents attended Sunday worship or meetings. This building was located across the street from the main sanctuary, a very convenient location. The classrooms accommodated some of the seven hundred children who attended our two Sunday schools each week. Upon completion of the building, these rooms were filled to capacity. This same phenomenon existed in another of the parishes. Yes, that is growth!

The Fish Market

One of the houses purchased near the church playground was named the Fish Market. This was a hangout place for the youth. The garage made a great gathering area for Saturday nights, and music groups would perform there. Singing could be heard up and down the block. This program would draw around one hundred youth from our church and their friends weekly.

Pastor Ollie Olson carried on a most successful evangelism program for youth. These meetings were appealing to young people in the area and a great Saturday evening outing! When I returned from college, this was a great place to meet up with friends.

EXTRAORDINARY PEOPLE IN MY LIFE

My fervent desire as a Christian was to be willing to spend any minute at any hour to reach people for the Lord and His Kingdom. As soon as I received the call for the ministry, it became clear to me that I should direct my whole ministry to that final goal. I have always believed in the reality of sin and grace, of obedience and disobedience, as well as heaven and hell. I wanted everyone to know what I knew—that you can have happiness now and forever.

With God's help, I have tried to use every good method: my family, every group possible, and even my vacation time to that end. "Serving wholeheartedly as if you were serving God, not men" (Ephesians 6).

One soul is worth the whole world

I discovered with *that* emphasis, my family received more of the desired good things in this world. I would never pit the wants of a needy soul against my faithfulness to my most wonderful wife and children. I have only pleasant memories of being a member for twenty-six years of Rotary International, which is one of the best service organizations for professionals. My wife and children became acquainted with the business world and professional people in our community through this group.

Bob Loranger

I have previously shared the story of my dear friend Bob Loranger, who graciously photographed my children's weddings. Here are stories of some of the other people who have shared their friendship and talents with me and my family over the years.

Joe Bowers, extraordinary hunter and fisherman

At a new mission, new to the ministry, and new to the culture of the West, I met Joe, who lived near our church. He was a modest, humble, and kind man. From him I not only learned the art of fishing in the river and hunting ducks and geese while lying on the ground in blinds in a field, but also how God turned his and his wife's lives around. They went from being just good, ordinary, quiet citizens to becoming a gloriously happy couple in the Lord. Joe, his wife, Bertha, and his mother lived across the street from us and became close friends. They also became adopted grandparents to our kids, which was a blessing since our biological family was a thousand miles away.

Don English, a volunteer director of stewardship

I will never forget the host of friends, leaders, and powerhouses in winning souls for Christ in the new, fast-growing church in South Sacramento, Gloria Dei Lutheran. May I tell you about at least one who called me because he knew I was available twenty-four hours a day when he had a family and marriage problem? We dealt immediately with his problem, and in this case it helped him out for many years.

Don was a born salesman and a people person. He became better than any other paid stewardship director we had, and he directed the financial part of an additional large school building of our new church. His children were enrolled in our school and Sunday school as well. He was a person who knew how to talk with everyone and understood them.

He loved boating, and some years later, when both of us were in the Los Angeles area, he invited Florence and me to be his first guests on his new two-bedroom, two-bath yacht, which had just arrived from Seattle.

By this time, some twenty years later, we had become close family friends (and remained so until he passed away prematurely after an organ transplant). He had continued in a business I had introduced to him, and now he had his own business with at least thirty employees. Even though my availability and my suggestions didn't amount to much, he graciously attributed his success to becoming a Christian, to our church, and to our own friendship. He also did significant financial work for Campus Crusade.

Have you spent a day at the state legislature?

I did, thanks to the Lord, and from my openness at all times to help James Wedworth, who called me many different times. James was a bicycle shop owner and Rotarian. He eventually took our ten-week membership inquiry class and became a fervent member and excellent resource for reaching people for our church. His whole family found Trinity Lutheran in Hawthorne a strong, fortifying power in their lives and especially in Jim's life in the political arena in Sacramento. I had the privilege of performing the marriages of a couple of his children. He also invited me to visit him in the state legislature, which was a thrill for me.

Bob, the man with the handlebar moustache

Bob Ward was not known as the most sanctified man on earth. We became acquaintances through some club work and then he called me about his approaching marriage. I told him frankly, but kindly, that I had one great request before I could even talk seriously about giving them premarital counseling. I suggested he and his fiancé enroll in our inquiry class to find out about our Savior and Lord. They did, and they finished the class and became committed members. These two rather tall, impressive professional people wanted to start teaching a new first grade Sunday school class for which there was a need. You can just imagine how the first graders' eyes opened wide when they first saw Bob with the handlebar moustache teaching their class. They were blessed to hear him speak with his unusual "golden tongue."

After I had left Hawthorne and was in Camarillo, he and his wife became trained and experienced in the Layman Evangelism Movement. They were a part of a six-couple team that came into our church and led a week of Evangelism Outreach. What a blessing Mr. and Mrs. Bob Ward had become to me as well as to many churches in the area, all because we had an immediate response program to them when they were in need.

How a navy captain influences pastors now

A man and his family found a new spiritual visibility by means of a structural liturgical service. He found that our church in Camarillo some thirty-five years ago fulfilled his needs by including all of the biblical and beautiful parts of his childhood liturgical church. This influenced him to join First Lutheran.

Dave was the key person a few years ago who discovered an extra $50,000 for our church. He found a renter—a school—that could use one-half of our large, empty school building, which was an answer to our church's financial needs until the time we could open up our own school.

This past year, he wrote a letter of recommendation for my first book, a guide to help pastors be successful in taking a strong hold of their jobs as administrators so that the Lord could prosper their churches and grow them. His letter was also included in the second printing of *The Pastor-Administrator: The Key to Growth and Vitality*. A copy of the letter is included in this book. His recommendation was most helpful, as he is a layperson in the Lutheran Church, plus he has the qualifications as an officer in charge of the helicopter unit here at the Port Hueneme base, as well as having been a naval officer in charge of our naval forces in Europe. His recommendation lent prestige to my book, due to his having had such influential positions in the past.

Incidentally, he was a golf partner of mine twenty-five years ago and has been again since we returned to Camarillo. Even as of this morning, he still is beating me rather soundly. The latter I don't like! But what a friend and man of God.

Recommendation by an awesome golfer and friend, Captain David Zinger

The Pastor-Administrator: The Key to Growth and Vitality
Pastor Hiepler,

This book is a must-read for all seminary students, new pastors, and those who are struggling in their careers.

As a former career naval officer, I remember, at the beginning of Aviation Officers Candidate School, how disappointed I was when the Marine Corps Drill Instructor said, "I know you guys came here thinking you would be wearing leather flight jackets with white scarves blowing in the wind. Well, let me tell you something; yes, you are here to train to be a coveted Naval Aviator, but you are to be an officer first and a pilot second." What I learned throughout my naval career was to be successful, you not only have to be a skilled pilot, but more importantly, you need to be an excellent administrator and leader of men. To be a successful administrator you need to know what to delegate and what not to delegate.

To be a successful pastor-administrator, you must practice what you are not good at. Like in any sport, you must put more time in the practice sessions to improve your weak areas. It doesn't improve your game if you spend most of your time practicing the things you are good at instead of those that you are not good at. Pastors need to practice being excellent administrators.

You can't grow if you are satisfied with the status quo or satisfied with the idea that it's always been that way. To be a successful pastor/leader, you must be innovative and be able to think "outside the box."

This is an excellent book. Thank you for giving me the opportunity to read it. I wouldn't change anything in it. Your friend, David Zinger

Have you known someone who has flown with Colonel Lindbergh? When serving the Lord, there are so many unexpected experiences and blessings given by God. I was asked to lead in a Sunday morning Bible class in 2011 at our church, Good Shepherd. I didn't want to be there alone nor have just a few attendees, so I placed an article in the newspaper called "The Starting of a New Bible Study." That Sunday, in walked a woman with a smile on her face, new to the church, with the article in her hand, which she had cut out of the local paper. Ann and her husband, Clyde, became my new best friends. I have received many very good ideas and encouragement for writing this book from this couple.

I have had a lifelong desire to know someone firsthand who could tell me more about the great Colonel Charles Lindbergh. I was only six years old when I heard of a man who had flown an airplane across the Atlantic Ocean alone. To me, it was almost like turning the earth upside down to even know a person who could fly an airplane. In 1926, being the only one in the plane and making that trip across the ocean was an unimaginable feat.

It was years later, when I was in grade school, that, if someone in our house heard an airplane overhead, he would call to everyone in the house, and we would all run out and look up and say, "Where?" Then the sound directed our sight to Mr. Canfield, who owned the plane— the only flying machine anyone had in Williston or in the area. After I finished three years of graduate school and before going out to my first job and settling down, I flew in an actual prop plane. Even when I went to the airport in Minneapolis to buy my ticket to Barksdale Field in Louisiana, the thought came to my mind, *I'd better be most prepared to go to heaven.*

After accidentally discovering that my new friend Clyde had flown with the great Colonel Charles Lindbergh, I realized that my lifelong wish was fulfilled. Not only had he copiloted a plane with Colonel Lindbergh, but my new friend had been in and out of the home of former president Harry Truman, the key man to end World War II in 1945.

Clyde invited by Lindbergh to be copilot

My friend Clyde had been a pilot since he was nineteen years of age. He had been a member of the Ferry Command during the war and had the privilege of flying many different types of airplanes. He met Colonel Lindbergh in Dearborn, Michigan, at the Willow Run Airport, home of the great B-29 airplane. As Lindbergh had been told that Clyde was an experienced pilot, he invited him on board and asked him to come up front and be the copilot. Clyde was invited to do this on several occasions when Colonel Lindbergh was at Willow Run.

My friend found Lindbergh to be a real gentleman but very much a private man. When I asked him if Lindbergh had shared any advice about flying, Clyde said that he told him after takeoff to always, always fly the airplane once around the airport to check that everything was in good working order before flying out of the area.

Clyde is a modest man, even at his advanced age of ninety-six, and has allowed me to use his first name only in my story. Believe it or not, his wife is now one of my most important editors and proofreaders for this book! God sure is full of unexpected surprises.

Ken Graham

I spent more than three hours on October 18, 2014, at the same lunch table, in the same chair, next to the same friend—Ken Graham. It seemed like just one hour. Don't you find that time flies when spending time with friends?

Ken and I have shared many commonalities during our great quarter-of-a-century friendship:

We're both from North Dakota.

He was president of the congregation and building committee when I was pastor in Camarillo.

He led a fund raiser for Ventura Lutheran High School, and I was on the board.

We attended college eighty miles apart.

Some of our children selected our alma maters for college.

Our wives are extraordinary leaders in our church and have happy, uplifting personalities everyone loves.

Both of us are serving the Lord, voluntarily, in our retirement, with a host of friends in our present church as well as in the national denomination of the AFLC.

Both of us are eager to assist in the growth of our congregation and to win souls for Christ and for eternity.

Pastor Ollie

March 5, 2014
Dear Orv,

I just wanted to drop a note and let you know how good it was to see you at the Home Missions conference in Phoenix last week. I didn't know you were going to be there, so it was a nice surprise to see you that first night.

I want to thank you for the copy of the book on the pastor-administrator that you so generously gave to all those in attendance there. That was very kind of you. I remember when you did that dissertation work, as it was my first year with you at Hawthorne, and you would sometimes take me to classes there at the California Graduate School of Theology, and I appreciated the opportunity to sit in.

The book is an excellent treatise of the opportunities and responsibilities in the area of pastor-administrator and can be an excellent guide for those who are just starting out in the ministry as well as for those who are veterans. I was only involved in a smaller area of responsibility, which you carried well during those years.

May God continue to grant you good health and strength in the days ahead.

Sincerely, Ollie Olson

Pastor Ollie was the most successful youth pastor in my entire ministry. He was one of four pastors at Trinity in Hawthorne. He left our church to be a full-time instructor in our California Lutheran Bible School in LA. During his time of four years in our church, we would have one hundred or more youth every Saturday night at our Fish Market (youth house).

Then and now, I know of no other Lutheran church where this many youth would gather weekly. Pastor Ollie is an excellent teacher and makes the Bible relevant. He had what it took to draw the youth and to keep them interested in coming.

Pastor Oliver Olson has been a very close friend and became a member or our Community Lutheran in Oceanside. This man has shed blessings on many!

MEDIOCRITY CAN'T MAKE ME A PRISONER— LESSONS FROM GUST AND ANNA

Mediocrity tries to wear me down and rob me of my dreams! With God's help, I will set goals to be among the best. He has given me His perfect Son, who lived here, died here, and rose from the ground here—my Savior, Lord, and King forever. I cannot be satisfied with less than the best. Can you?

I won't be satisfied with being just an average son!

I won't be satisfied with being just an average father!

I won't be satisfied with being just an average husband!

I won't be satisfied with being just an average employer!

I won't be satisfied with being just an average investor!

I won't be satisfied with being just an average basketball player!

I won't be satisfied with being just an average church member!

I won't be satisfied with being just an average tither!

I won't be satisfied with being just an average pastor!

Average is not anything to brag about, considering a recent definition that is flying around these days: "Average on a chart is the worst of all the best. Average on a chart is best of all the worst."

Even at the age of ninety-four, the Lord has inspired me so that mediocrity cannot rob me of my dreams and new adventures. How many more months or years I have, I don't know! That, too, is in the Lord's hands. Romans 8:28 says, "And we know that in all things God works for the good of those who love him, who have been called according to his purpose."

I won't be satisfied with being just an average son. My mother and father were my example of having the maximum amount of respect, honor, and appreciation for hardworking parents. My mother's and father's parents were all born in Germany and came to this country to give their children more than they could ever have had by just staying in Germany and being among the average. My dad left the comforts of Minnesota and launched out at age twenty-one to North Dakota and became a homesteader with all of its trials.

I am not satisfied with being the average father. I should ask my children to honestly write in here all my failures. I can tell you my dad was a great example as a father. Even though he would have said the things he did were ordinary, all of us six children found him far beyond the ordinary.

He was, as I recall, a most sacrificial father for all of his children. He and Mother wanted the best education for their children, even if it often meant giving up some comforts. They started, as I recall, by establishing and finding local grade schools. They were one of the four couples responsible for moving the grammar school building from about four miles away to within just over a mile of our home. Dad continued to go beyond average by taking Gertie, my older sister, to Ellendale, North Dakota, to college in 1928–1929. Most of our friends and relatives were comfortable with only having a high-school education. I recall seeing my dad and Gertie leaving in our 1926 Chevy, with Grandma's big trunk strapped onto the back bumper of the car. The trunk was big enough for all of Gertie's earthly belongings. Incidentally, this trunk went with several of us to college, and now it is carefully preserved in my new shed here at the end of the carport at my home. Grandma had bought it for her trip back to Iowa to see Uncle Carl, her oldest son.

Dad's famous phrase when his son would ask him, "How's it going?" was "*Es muss gehen!*" (It must go). Thus he worked more than the average man to farm more land than what the average farmer would be happy with. When things were difficult, he wouldn't easily give up and be average. His famous saying was: "There is more than one way to skin a cat."

He had a hired man every spring and several in the fall. I recall two things that hired men would say: "Gust really makes us work from sunup to sundown, and he works right with us. In spite of that, he is so thankful to us whenever we do more than the average and shows us appreciation when it's all done."

I am not satisfied with being the average investor. Not exactly my field, but the little I have done has been fun in following the example of my dad, his dad, and Pastor Ed Astrup (my good friend from college). Properties, especially land, will not fail as investments, especially land in California in the good times.

I am not satisfied with being the average basketball player. I am different from my son and two grandsons and granddaughter in two ways: First, I never touched a basketball until I was a freshman in high school. Second, Mark, and now the grandsons, have been better than average, and we are expecting fabulous results from Ryan and Paul next year. In my case, the only plus was that I held in there even until my last game in my last year in high school. We had lost in the semifinal and played the consolation game that determined third and fourth place in the tournament, when something unusual happened: I played my best game of the whole season. They must have judged from the last game because I was selected as one of the best ten of ten teams in the county! I was the only one from my team who was called up onstage, with nine other players from other teams.

Florence has taught me to be more than a casual friend or church member. Tithing is being only average. The great road machine manufacturer and founder R. G. LeTourneau has taught me to set my goal of keeping 10 percent and giving away 90 percent. I have a good start toward that. Some years are much better than others.

As a pastor, it's only average to sustain membership and keep everyone happy. It's not very average to have only two hundred in a congregation in California. I have learned this by having five parishes in

California. You need at least three hundred members to maintain a building; pay for a pastor's salary, housing, and staffing; pay for leadership in youth work and music; and be part of a worldwide mission effort.

"And know His will and approve of what is superior, because you are instructed by the law; if you are convinced that you are a guide for the blind a light for those who are in the dark" (Romans 2:18–19). Jesus also said, "I will give you life and give it more abundantly" (John 10:10). Yes, the Lord is always here to give and to motivate us to give excellence abundantly.

CHAPTER 11

TRANSITIONS

LIFE BEGINS AT NINETY

For two days, it appeared to be ending

Being seventy and then eighty years old was good, but I knew there was still room for new opportunities and new adventures. Opportunities that were totally unexpected and some say "successful and extraordinary" in many ways. My ninetieth year had two very opposite experiences.

"The Righteous call out and the Lord hears" (Psalm 34:17).

First, let me tell you about the most glorious and exciting celebration that anyone, even younger people, could have experienced. It took place on February 7, 2010, three days before my ninetieth birthday. It was planned by our three children as Florence's and my sixty-fifth wedding anniversary *and* the sixty-fifth year of my ordination. I had discouraged the family from even mentioning my birthday. My golf-club buddies would probably throw the name back in the hat if they drew a ninety-year-old partner, even though I had shot my age twice the year before.

Mark and Michelle convinced me to have dinner at their house on the seventh for my birthday celebration. I wanted it to also be a consolidating event for two congregations who would be reunited after having been separated for at least eight years. This process of coming back together had been progressing successfully (described in another chapter in this book) for some weeks, but this would be the first big step physically.

It goes without saying that anything our three kids planned, and especially having it at Mark and Michelle's home, would be outstanding. This would be a great gathering of over one hundred friends, family, and church members. Florence and I still traveled the 165 miles frequently to attend both churches and especially for this event.

We were met at the gate with valet parking, and a wonderful dinner was served with great fellowship and visiting with so many dear people. Choirs from both churches sang, people spoke, and we were elated to have such a great homecoming. Our precious Michelle and Mark served 120 people for dinner and organized the program, at which time I had the unique opportunity of addressing the two churches as one. What a privilege it was to have the First Lutheran Choir perform, directed by Mr. Bill Minea, and to see in the choir the last remaining charter members of First Lutheran Church, Mr. and Mrs. Louie Vang. Not only were they charter members of First Lutheran, but she was the first preschool director of our school located at the front of the church property.

The organist, Mary, and her husband gave Florence and me the nicest hand-embroidered towel with our names on it in honor of our sixty-five years of ministry. The Good Shepherd Choir sang as well, and Pastor Jim Johnson gave a greeting. It was a most enjoyable afternoon for Florence and me.

At this time, we had no idea what would be happening in the coming months, as we were so excited about this occasion and also some other opportunities. Yes! It was happening at Gloria Dei Lutheran Church in

Sacramento, the congregation we started. Many from the congregation had contacted me to help them revive their church. This congregation had had a tough time with a leader and now really needed some direction to stay a Bible-centered church with good leadership. Together with friends from our Camarillo church, I visited Sacramento. We had a dinner for many of our old friends and members to reach out to them to see if a new church could be started. This new congregation could be combined with Gloria Dei and revive it, similar to what had happened in Camarillo.

About the same time I made a trip to the Bay Area for the funeral of my close friend, Pastor Magnus Anderson, who had died just after his one-hundredth birthday. We had celebrated his birthday a few months earlier. We had been together in many ventures throughout our ministry and would meet for golf on free days. The women would shop, and the men would golf and talk about new opportunities. Mag had supported us and also wanted to get a new church going in the Tulare area of California some years before, but the area was not conducive to beginning one. Mag was a great friend, colleague, and mentor.

Ninety years of age? Sixty-five years of marriage and of ministry? Where did the time go? What an experience, for which I will always be so thankful!

June of 2010

That June, our church convention was held at our AFLC church headquarters in Plymouth, Minnesota. This was only ten minutes from Dorene and Curt's home in Golden Valley. This was a great opportunity for Florence and me to attend the convention and also visit our kids. At that time it was already difficult for Florence to travel, but all went well. She stayed with Dorene while I attended the convention. We also had time to travel up to the Brainerd area, where our granddaughter Rachel worked and lived. We met her soon-to-be husband Matt and saw the house they were about to purchase. Such fun for us! The morning we were to leave for home, my nephew and his wife visited with us.

Dorene and Curt, as well as Dale and Audrey, noticed something a little different about my demeanor. Probably just the traveling had made me a little tired. They helped us at the airport with suitcases and a wheelchair for Florence, as I was a little confused and soon we were on our way home. As we came home, I enjoyed the catch-up of mowing both our lawns at home in Fallbrook and at our rental in Valley Center. This was always good exercise for me. As I was mowing the large lawn area in Valley Center, our next-door neighbor, Mrs. Peterson, came out to talk to Florence while she waited in the car. Mrs. Peterson would always warn me to take it easy when cutting the grass.

Something happened!
Florence and I returned home, which was a fifteen-minute drive for us from Valley Center. I acted normally, as far as I knew. I apparently called my doctor in San Diego, who was about an hour away, and made an appointment to see him the same day. I don't remember making the call. I really wanted to get an OK from the doctor to head to Sacramento to help out there for a few months in the Gloria Dei congregation.

I recall nothing from this time, even after four years. Everything is a void. The next part has been told to me.

I drove us down to Scripps Green for my appointment to see the doctor. Florence could no longer drive but always rode along with me and would wait in the car. She would read or take a nap while I was at an appointment. I had parked and entered on the hospital side, and once in, I had been directed to go to the urgent care area of the hospital. This office visit lasted two hours, as the doctor had discovered something was wrong. I was acting very "out of it," he said. He knew our granddaughter, Natalie Fox, worked there at the hospital, so he tried to get hold of her. She had just left for home but got a call to return to the hospital. Upon her arrival, she wondered where Florence was. They searched and found out that she was in the car on the other side of the hospital. Supposedly I had come out to tell her that my appointment would be lasting longer than expected. The doctor sent me for a scan;

Natalie brought Florence into the hospital and stayed with her and also called Ilene and Mark. I was immediately admitted.

Our precious granddaughter, Natalie, was a nurse there, but before her promotion she had been in charge of the nurses on the floor to which I was admitted. Everyone knew Natalie. Mark came, and Ilene took care of Florence. Dorene arrived soon after. Dorene and Ilene made not only medical decisions, which were primary, but also decisions about a host of other things that pertained to our home in Fallbrook—bill paying, my office, properties, tenants taken care of, and lawn service organized. The most important thing was to be there for Florence. Jim Fox picked up family from the airport and also helped out with business items. Everyone was involved. Living longer means a person may have more investments and business, but my kids took care of everything.

They call me Rip Van Winkle!

I was completely unaware of any of this and was totally "out of it" for four days.

When I awakened, I couldn't figure out why Nicole and her daughter, Gracie, from North Carolina were at my bedside, as well as Rachel from Minnesota, Amy from Washington, Jenna from Ohio, and Kari from Orange County, together with other grandchildren and family members. I am told that I didn't respond for many hours after the surgery, and when I did wake up, I'd just lain there and smiled but didn't say a word.

The good thing is I had no concern about anything. The great Dr. Sanchez had performed a successful surgery on a subdural hematoma in my brain. I had no concern about where my wife was, where the car was, or anything. I was in excellent hands, and I didn't even know it! As each day passed, I began saying more words and responding to what people said.

In a few days, the doctor gave me a good report. The bleeding had stopped with no seizures, and maybe if all went well, I could leave the hospital in a couple days. I was in the hospital for a total of seven days.

Weeks later, I remembered I had hit my head on the trunk of my new car a couple of times when I mistakenly hit the wrong part of the remote, and it popped open quickly.

The first big change at ninety years old

I needed rehabilitation, and inasmuch as I was Florence's main caregiver, we both had to leave our home in Fallbrook where we had been so happy. Everything we owned and loved was in that house in a great community, with views of two fairways of the Golf Club of California in Sycamore Ranch estates—one behind us and one across the street from our front door. We were only two houses from the golf clubhouse, putting greens, and driving range. We had lived in this house for only seven years, surrounded by a host of friends and fellow golfers from around the area. We were also not far from our great church, Community Lutheran. Dear friends such as the Hands and the Anthonsons were also nearby. Unfortunately, we needed to leave there to be cared for after my surgery. Our daughters, son, and daughter-in-law made the move to Camarillo possible. We were going home after twenty years.

At last, normal abilities return

My abilities returned after a few months, and I could soon make decisions on my own again. Thank you, Lord.

There was no question that Michelle and Mark's good suggestion to spend some time at AlmaVia in Camarillo was a great decision regarding all of our needs. We welcomed that, even if it should have to be a permanent move. AlmaVia is an assisted-living community, where I had my rehabilitation. The place was owned by Lutherans and Catholics. I had not heard of that type of ownership before. We were given great care and had good food and also space to entertain family and friends when they came to visit.

Our lives had been and would always be dedicated to the Lord's will, even though it included large changes. We loved Paul's word, "For it is God who works in you to will and to act in order to fulfill His good purposes" and "Do everything without grumbling or arguing" (Philippians 2:13–14). I like the fifteenth verse as well, even if it doesn't apply now: "Then you will shine among them as stars in the sky as you hold firmly to the Word of Life. I will be able to boast on that day of Christ that I did not run in vain or labor in vain."

Jesus heals bodies. As I saw promises of God's healing taking place, I am reminded of Psalm. 103:2–4 that I'd learned in an OT Bible class taught in our public high school. "Bless the Lord oh my soul and forget not all of His benefits, who forgives all your sins and heals all of your diseases. Who redeems your life, who satisfies your desires with good things so that your youth is renewed like the eagle's."

Maybe life doesn't begin at ninety?

In November 2010, we moved into our newly renovated house, which I had found in the beautiful Adolfo Mobile Estates in Camarillo. It is everything anyone could ever want, including everything we will ever need.

This whole change was made possible because Ilene and Dorene helped me do all that was necessary to sell, sort, pack, and give away things in our house in Fallbrook. They helped make it possible to rent it out immediately.

Naomi and Jeri, our friends from church who had worked for me in caregiving, became our angels in moving us from AlmaVia. They arranged and moved boxes and got us settled in our mobile home. Naomi, who is a very feminine young woman and not tall in stature, had taken weight lifting and had EMT training. She moved and placed furniture. She also went with me the 165 miles to our old house and helped prepare items there. I had my dear friends the McMillens working to get a moving company in place. Everyone worked together.

At ninety years old, I made the move with less-than-normal stress or fuss. Not only that, but the move to "the trailer" of nineteen hundred square feet cost us only a tenth of the price of a regular house, plus it is so roomy and spacious that we have been able to entertain friends there for our apple-pie-and-ice-cream socials and other special events and family gatherings.

Apple-pie-and- ice-cream socials

After moving into our new home in the Adolfo Estates, we thought it would be a great idea to meet some of our neighbors and renew acquaintances. This was also a good time to have a special speaker or theme for the event and invite people for Sunday afternoon fellowship. Some people come to know Christ Jesus as their Lord and Savior through these events. We have ample parking across the street as well as in our driveway and can have up to sixty-five people attend. These events could not be done without the hospitality and party-planning expertise of Bev and Jane and their group of friends, and the Zingers, Mineas, Schmidts, Langness, Divits, and others. They come up with a theme, purchased the apple pies and ice cream, and elegantly served the food. They have been key people in fulfilling our purpose for the gatherings.

Our guests came from San Diego as well as Davis and Sacramento areas. We renewed friendships as well as met people in our community while sharing the gift of love, which our Lord has given to us. I have learned so much from the various speakers we have had. Following are some of the fine people with whom we've shared fellowship.

Barbara Cameron, author of *A Full House of Growing Pains*, neighbor, and friend. The Camerons are the parents of Kirk Cameron from *Growing Pains, Fireproof, Left Behind*, and many other movies. Their daughter is Candace Cameron-Bure, producer, author, inspirational speaker, and actress who has appeared in *Full House, Dancing with the Stars*, and many more shows.

Kenneth McMillen, a friend, former parishioner, and high-school teacher; he walked from Mexico to Canada and shared his adventure of climbing Mount Kilimanjaro.

Warren Willis, a former parishioner and longtime friend, founder and CEO of high-school Bible clubs in Southern California, and leader of a mission surge in the Mongolia, Asia Campus Crusade for forty-plus years.

Pastor Robert Bradberry, son-in-law married to daughter Ilene, a pastor at the fifty-thousand-member Saddleback Christian church in Lake Forest, California. Under the leadership of Campus Crusade, he was in Africa for fourteen years.

Sharon Herbst Carlson, who shared her musical talents and gifts. She grew up at Trinity in Hawthorne and was a friend of Nelene's. Our families have been close friends for fifty years.

Musical miniconcerts by the Kilpatrick family singers and other friends and family add to the afternoon entertainment at our Apple Pie and Ice Cream gatherings.

Good Times with Friends

ROOTED IN FAITH CAMPAIGN

June 2009–September 2012

The great recession, the global economic decline in the first decade of the 2000s, brought distress to many churches and private schools. Weekly worship service attendance dropped significantly at many churches, and many of those churches that had schools experienced a large drop in enrollment. Trinity Lutheran in Hawthorne, California, was among those. Families moved their children from costly private schools into free public schools. The effects of this economic downturn had a continuous influence into 2014.

So how did Trinity cope with such dramatic declines? How did Trinity keep from closing the school?

The following is a brief history of one of the most dynamic and successful fund-raising campaigns in the history of our church. Current members, former members, and friends of Trinity from around the country participated in a three-plus-year endeavor to save our day school from potential closure and to establish an excellent outreach program in our community.

Day-school history

From 1960 to 2003, Trinity Day School prospered. Over those fifty-five years, enrollment was maintained well above two hundred students and early on up to five hundred students. We were very comfortable with things.

In 2004, enrollment began dropping. We had experienced a few ups and downs over the years before, but it wasn't until 2006 that we found a very disturbing trend had been developing. By 2006, enrollment was dropping more quickly than before.

By 2007, things were looking pretty grim. Enrollment continued to drop. Many private schools in the area were closing. But Trinity's congregation refused to budge on their commitment to offset lost tuition.

Their commitment to keep this important outreach ministry alive and to keep the school open was a priority.

In 2007, we began an aggressive marketing program to the community. We held meetings and listened to what our school parents told us. Significant research and planning took place as a result of the meetings.

By 2008, the congregation approved additional expenditure for a computer lab.

As we entered 2009, the very existence of Trinity Lutheran Day School was coming under question. Should the school reduce the number of grades offered? Should the school close as many others had? There was no question that Trinity Lutheran could not continue to sustain the school financially without doing significant financial harm to the church as a whole.

Throughout this time, Trinity families and others offered abundant prayers and sacrifices. Our country had entered into a very deep and damaging period of recession.

Trinity Lutheran had taken a stand against closing the school and had done about all it could do. God had put our church to the test, and we had stayed the course. Now, God was about to reveal the rest of His plan.

The Rooted in Faith campaign

The following was submitted by John Brewer.

One day in March 2009, Pastor Orville Hiepler (pastor from 1960–1978) and John Brewer (church president) met at an unrelated event at Trinity and were casually discussing the plight of the school. Pastor Larry Becker joined in additional discussions where a possible new fund-raising campaign at Trinity was considered. A committee was formed to further evaluate the concept. The committee and Pastor Hiepler presented to the council and the congregation. The ideas were approved by the church council.

The campaign was given the name Rooted in Faith (affectionately called RIF). The acting RIF committee was formalized, consisting of Shirley Becker, John Brewer, Janet Johnson, Shelly Effler, and Scott Abukoff. Dhirley Rickard and Susan Newsom joined the committee. A kickoff dinner was held June 28, 2009, with attorney Mark Hiepler, an alumnus of the school, speaking.

The campaign got off to a quick start, and God's hand was very apparent from the beginning. We had no idea how exciting and successful this campaign was about to become.

In summary, the day school was saved. By 2012, all K–8 classes were once again being offered, and the school was growing once again. Some solid church outreach programs were instituted, in particular the Alpha Program under the leadership of Rich and Janet Johnson.

An amount of $122,000 was received through donations during this three-year period. Many updates and ministries started at Trinity during this time. What a blessing.

The RIF campaign was formally closed with a large catered celebration and thanksgiving dinner event on September 29, 2012. At this time, Pastor Hiepler's name was placed in the Trinity Hall of Fame.

After such an exciting time for our church, the leadership decided to begin an additional fund-raising event following the closing of the RIF campaign. This campaign is called Faith at Work and includes sanctuary refurbishing, sound system updates, and some new signage. At this writing, $88,000 has been raised for this campaign.

Praise God from whom all blessings flow!

CHAPTER 12

FEELING AND STAYING YOUNG

TIPS FOR STAYING YOUNG AT NINETY-FOUR

Activities

People have asked me, "Where do you get the energy for doing all you do?"

First of all, being active is in my genes, and I began many of my activities at a younger age and have continued them throughout my life.

I especially enjoy things like playing golf, which keeps me from being lazy. During my Hawthorne days, I usually played early in the morning so it would not interfere with work. It got me out of bed and ready for the day. My friend Don and I would head out in the early morning and would be on the tee box before the sun was up. We could get in at least nine holes before we had to be at our respective offices for work.

Attending two Bible studies on Wednesdays, being a part of my church in Camarillo, and attending multiple events including anniversaries and weddings has kept me busy socializing and in contact with our many friends. Find a need in life and fulfill it.

Take classes

Never wait until you can find time or wait until retirement to exercise. I do stretching exercises each morning before getting out of bed. Walking and enjoying God's great creation is another form of keeping healthy and staying young. If you wait for a convenient time, there is the danger that you'll never start a good exercise regimen. The hardest part is getting started. Develop a frame of mind so you find ways to enjoy exercise. Competing against yourself or improving a skill is advantageous. If you are used to walking in a certain direction, change it and walk in a different direction. It helps clear out the brain cobwebs. I'm always thinking of ways to improve and to make my exercise enjoyable. The Lord knows I need improvement in all my efforts.

There are so many classes available through community education, health centers, or in your very own fifty-five-and-over community. Right now, at ninety-five, I attend a class at our own center here in Adolfo Estates Park. We have an excellent teacher who knows the art of teaching to an older age group. She makes us feel comfortable doing low-impact exercise whether sitting in a chair or standing beside it. She stresses the importance of taking deep breaths and thinking about our body as it moves. It is also free for those who live in the park. I attend for thirty minutes a day, twice a week.

Physical and occupational therapy is a good way to get into exercise. Knee strengthening and going with Florence to therapy has given me some good insights. This past year I have worked on getting rid of an extra ten pounds that somehow crept up on my middle area. I'm happy to say that I won't have to discard several trousers that had become too tight because over the last few months I have dropped eight pounds. Many times I have skipped a full lunch and had a piece of fruit or toast instead. I also golf twice a month, and the days I don't have a class, I go for a walk or have a game, or I will go to the range and hit a bucket or two of golf balls.

Exercise is so important to me, physically and mentally. Speaking with a loud, strong voice, memorizing numbers and Bible verses, holding my head up high, and smiling often makes me look better and feel better.

Younger friends—what a blessing!
The credit goes to my dad and mom.

My dad taught me by example by lending machinery to a neighbor who had not prepared himself for a "rainy day." The younger, neighboring farmer had not taken care of his machinery, so when the time came to harvest and his machines were broken and rundown, my dad stepped in to help out, not expecting anything in return. My dad mentored him and explained how to store machinery and the proper care of it, and these men became lasting friends. It would be like helping someone on skid row or the homeless of larger cities. We have known people who, through the help of concerned, caring people, have been restored to their own families. My dad was one who loved helping the "down and outer," and it made him more thankful that he could be the giver rather than having to be the receiver. I have followed in his footsteps and love the giving; it is enjoyable and fulfilling. I do find it difficult at times to be the receiver!

My mother was always friends with people her children's age. She would invite them to meals or bring them delicious cookies, and they, in turn, loved to help her out and be a part of her family. They had a special bond. This widened her scope of friends. She also enjoyed visiting "the old folks" in the nursing home, even at the age of eighty-five. To this day, when I call my friend Mary, she will say, "Is this Anna's son?" Mary is twenty years younger than I and quilted with my mother when she was in her twenties.

Back to the enjoyment of having younger friends, I receive much from two couples: one of them only twenty years younger and the other forty years younger. I have been blessed with an array of friends of all ages through being in church work, so it is a blessing to be acquainted with the other generations. I am so thankful for a younger friend who calls to see if I'd like to golf every couple of weeks.

Others stop by with a meal or sweets. My son's parents-in-law, Renee and Carl, will come by with a meal to share. Involvement in grandchildren's activities, such as going to basketball games, plays, awards, and meeting their friends, has been a wonderful thing since moving back to Camarillo. Communicating by phone with grandchildren living a distance away helps me think outside of my little world and forces me to try to stay up with the times. Friends from Sacramento and Hawthorne have kept in contact throughout the years, and now some have gone on to Glory, but their children stay connected to me by visits and letters. Joyce and Bob Borrud visit frequently from Sacramento. They are much appreciated, and I am grateful for my friends of all ages.

As I look back again on my parents, I see so many ways that I have tried to follow them and their example. The church and the fellowship and friendships I have made brought these people into my life.

Accepting unusual opportunities

Many unbelievable things happened during 2014. My daughters and son and many of my close friends encouraged me to write a book, so that is what I did. During this same period of time in 2013 and 2014, I was unusually blessed with opportunities to speak at our Bible school and seminary in Minneapolis and lecture to a seminary class Practical Theology, namely stewardship. This was followed with speaking on my previous book, which was a gift to each pastor at a Home Mission Institute in Phoenix, Arizona, in February of 2014.

Traveling in summer 2014 to two speaking engagements helped me to stay relevant. It was very hard work preparing for these engagements, as I was out of practice from delivering weekly sermons and Bible studies. I had an invitation to speak near my parental home at a family Bible camp as well as one to speak at Florence's home church in Tioga, North Dakota. I think they got to the bottom of the barrel when it came to choosing a speaker for those events, but I am always looking for more opportunities.

It would have been easy for me to refuse. I know I could have found some good, believable excuses, such as "traveling is not as easy as it used to be"; however, I can blame my dad and mother for not declining. They taught me by example: "Never refuse an opportunity to help someone if at all possible." I also continue to praise God for all He has given me and to tell others of His love for us.

Why celebrate my parents' 104th wedding anniversary?
You may ask the above question, and why would I celebrate it in 2014? The Tioga speaking engagement was at the time of my parents' wedding anniversary. Interesting timing. Not much has been mentioned about their anniversary since 1970, when my parents celebrated their sixtieth. My dad had become ill a few days before we were to celebrate. We followed through with the plans and decided to celebrate it in August, as that is when most of the family could attend a celebration for my parents. We had the entire celebration taped, and we took it to the hospital for Dad to see. His relatives from Minnesota had come especially for this significant occasion and went up to the hospital to see him. At that time, even though he had some serious limitations, we expected him to be home in a few days. That did not happen. I came back to North Dakota a couple of weeks later for his funeral, as did a number of relatives who had just attended the anniversary.

The friends and relatives had come from far and wide for this celebration, as had been the case only ten years before when we celebrated their fiftieth anniversary. It was at that celebration that Gilmore (my sister's husband) and his father came driving up in an old touring car from the '20s. He gave my mom and dad a ride around the community.

A wedding celebration on June 1 was also very significant for another reason, especially for Gertie and Gilmore (my sister and her husband), inasmuch as they were married on our parents' anniversary, June 1, 1937, at the church parsonage in Epping, North Dakota. We had a large reception for all of the families and relatives from both sides out at our home farm.

Yes, I too wondered why I was privileged to go back to North Dakota in 2014, and why I would be asked to speak on Sunday, June 1, in Tioga, where Florence and I were married sixty-nine years ago on August 22, 1945. Pastor Richard Carr of Zion Lutheran asked me some months ago if I would speak at the Sunday worship in the Grain Farm Festival Building on that particular Sunday and have a Bible study on Saturday the day before. These two services would conclude a four-day evangelism crusade conducted by Zion Lutheran as outreach to the community and the oil workers.

So why, after more than twenty years, was I asked to return to my roots and have two opportunities to share God's Word? Our daughter, Nelene, who is now in heaven, used to like the saying, "There are no coincidences with the Lord." Nothing has made me happier than to go back to the area from which Florence and I had received so much and share the Evangel, the Good News of salvation, and to point people to an eternity with Him forever! I don't know of any place in the world I would rather have been invited. I'm looking forward to possibly going back to the area again, if the Lord wills and health permits, to get a building project progressing. I mentioned to these people that there aren't many things at which I feel that I am an expert, but I do have confidence in how to go about a building program, having had two experiences in the past eight years plus several major building programs throughout my ministry.

Camp experience

Going home to North Dakota as an invited guest Bible study teacher at the Upper Missouri Ministries family Bible camp was a thrill. This camp is located only five miles from my boyhood farm, twenty miles northeast of Williston, between Springbrook and Epping. What a treat that I could get back to my roots, which has happened infrequently in the last twenty years.

I have remained eternally thankful for all of the positive influences I remember from Springbrook, Epping, Wheelock, Ray, Tioga, and the county seat of Williston. I can think of nothing I would rather do than to share the knowledge of the joyous life from receiving the Lord that I had through my parents, pastors, schoolmates, and friends during the first twenty-five years of my life.

It delighted my heart to use that time to show my gratitude to the children and grandchildren of my fellow classmates as well as former neighbors who meant so much to me through the years. I enjoyed seeing many relatives, who were scattered throughout the area, as well as business friends, attorneys, and church friends whom I have had numerous contacts with through the years.

The culminating event was a church service followed by the annual corn feed and quilt auction, attended by seven hundred people from the community. Nieces Gayle and Gloria and nephews Arlan, Bruce, and Todd joined us for the celebration. Former friends and students of Florence's came up to express to me what a wonderful teacher and beautiful person Florence was. One lady said that she would never forget the glow on Florence's face when she came into the classroom wearing her engagement ring for the first time. The area of the Upper Missouri Bible Camp was also the place where I was first introduced to Florence by a mutual friend, Hazel Soiseth, who had attended my high school for two years and finished her high school years with Florence in Tioga.

Adding to the enjoyment was having Ilene and Dorene with me at camp. We had a beautiful room, private bath, and large windows looking out on the windswept prairies. This was in the retreat center and only steps from where I led two Bible studies during this family camp. The food service was excellent, and they had a golf cart available for traveling to and from the meals or for just taking in this beautiful campus.

This Bible camp had a special attachment for my whole family inasmuch as my dad, Gust Hiepler, helped build it. This was also where the small creek, which was dammed up by the government during the Great Depression of the '30s, is located. My dad worked for the WPA and had a four-horse team and Fresno scraper, helping to build it into what would eventually be a recreational area for the community. About eight years after all of this, my dad and others in the congregation concluded that this area would be a great place for a camp, and in 1946, they helped with moving the church building from Springbrook to the lake-dam area two miles away. (The church had been closed, as most of the people began attending church in Epping.) A former creamery, St. James Lutheran Church became the main gathering place for the Bible camp. This now is the dining hall.

At this time we were privileged to dedicate the Hiepler Lodge, a twenty-four-person cottage for campers to stay in during their camp time. Bible camps have always had a special place in my heart. The Bible camp experience that I had had at Metigoshe while in high school was the foundation for the work I have been doing for all of my life.

We did go back to my farmstead where I grew up. The house is gone, but we were able to visit my nephew, who has built a beautiful place on the prairie in the same place I had spent many hours playing as a child, riding my horse Blacky, and helping with farm chores! Jeff and Heather are now enjoying their beautiful prairie home as Mom and Dad enjoyed their homestead shack in 1910.

Returning to my roots caused me to praise God. He said, "Then if you declare with your mouth, Jesus is Lord and believe in your heart that God raised Him from the dead, you will be saved" (Romans 10:9). What a privilege He gives us when we can proclaim His Word.

AN EXTRAORDINARY DAY

Recently, my son and daughter-in-law invited me to a party that they were hosting. It was a Christian substitute for what many others were doing near Halloween as well as a chance to celebrate Michelle's fiftieth birthday!

Instead of ghosts, skeletons, and devils, Michelle had asked everyone to dress up as a historical figure. I chose to be a patriotic statesman. I knew that instead of alcoholic beverages, they would have coolers filled with Cokes, 7-Ups, and fruit juices, which would be all around their little theater as well as the recreation room.

I was puzzled by what to wear and who to pretend to be. I wanted to add to the fun of the night and not to subtract from it by sitting near the TV acting like I was too old to participate. If you are over seventy-five, you know what I am talking about. However, it became easy and took only a few minutes to enter into the spirit of the celebration. The thing that took the most time was getting into a mind-set that would gear me toward the fun rather than searching for a way to be excused.

Life sparkles with unknown events

Our houses contain so many things that can be repurposed without any expense or hours of shopping. I proved this to be true by piecing together a costume without any expense involved. I got the inspiration, perhaps, because Michelle and Mark had set the stage. I knew that whatever they planned would be great fun for everyone, from their teenage children's younger friends to friends nearer my age. I thought of a man—a patriot, dude, cowboy, rancher—who later became president of the United States. Above all, he was a rancher in my home state near Medora, North Dakota. He was known for his charge up San Juan Hill during the Cuban invasion as well as organizing his Rough Riders and being one of those who opened the West for immigrants and others who were settling in these parts of our great country. His fabulous, exciting, and adventurous life is depicted daily each year in a great outdoor amphitheater from June through September in Medora, North Dakota. Every time we go back by car to our old stomping grounds in the Williston area, we plan a day and night stop at Medora, and each time we become more excited about "how the West was won."

It is an exciting way of reviewing our history of celebrities made famous by serving their country and serving other people in various ways.

Guess who the dude is?
I immediately found a tie, a western cowboy hat, a fake moustache, and glasses, which were all lying around, hardly ever used. My UPS man quickly made a simple sign to hang around my neck that said, "Guess Who? Dude, Patriot, Rancher, and Cowboy," to which I added, "If you only take a guess, you'll get one kiss. Guess who I am, you'll get five kisses!" My pocket was full of chocolate kisses.

Seldom have I had as much fun as I had that night. Having my picture taken with my daughter, Ilene, as she posed as the US flag designer Betsy Ross, and with Ilene's daughter, Kari, dressed as famous Mexican artist Frida Kahlo, was a highlight!

Everyone who attended, from teenager through the ninety-four-year-old, not only enjoyed it but will look back on that evening as extraordinary.

The whole night also demonstrated how to provide homemade fun for the young and old instead of always going out somewhere. Mark and Michelle are so hospitable, and they use their home as a great gathering place to entertain friends and family!

CONTRASTS IN MY LIFE

The contrasts are so extreme for me at ninety-four years of age that I can hardly believe them myself. The first is that, basically, for the last twenty-five years, though retired from a regular parish ministry, I need no paycheck. I do receive a normal pastor's retirement pension and

Social Security. Neither is large, but with other God-given, undeserved windfalls, I am comfortable. Life is good. This alone would not keep me "refired" and eager to get up every morning. As I have mentioned other places in this book, no one could have more unexpected, unusual, and very special opportunities than I have daily. I was able to start three new churches from scratch and serve another without pay for ten years. Also, during these twenty-five years, I have served as an interim pastor for a few weeks in North Dakota, Wisconsin, and Tennessee. In addition to that, I have worked as a consultant for churches that weren't just on a plateau, but in decline. With God's help, I have had considerable success, allowing me to continue being a blessing to others. Trinity Lutheran School and Church have been generous beyond my belief. They called me back a couple of years after a program I had suggested had been successful, and they had an evening of celebration when they placed my name in their Hall of Fame, at the age of ninety-one.

A second big contrast in my life has been to be with my wonderful son, his most valued family, and my much-beloved church here in Camarillo during the past four years. I couldn't appreciate anything more than moving back to Camarillo. Florence and I miss our home in Fallbrook, but we experienced three happy years living together in our own home at Adolfo Park in Camarillo. It all began with our moving to AlmaVia, an assisted-living facility here. I had just had a serious surgery in June of 2010, and Florence had had a minor stroke a few years earlier, so this temporary home worked well for a few months. I told people after I had recovered 75 percent that this was such a nice place to stay, and we could stay there for the rest of our lives, but it was for older people! Seriously, it was a value judgment on my part as to whether we stayed there or moved to our own home. I would have saved some hard work getting our present place in livable condition, especially up to all of the good codes in this excellent park, if AlmaVia had been the right place for us at that time.

There is one great contrast to all of these things: after my nightly enjoyable visit for a couple of hours with Florence, going home *alone* is so difficult. When I get into my car and drive the eight minutes home, *I cry out loud like a baby.*

I feel terrible coming home when Florence is not here. I am crying out loud now, alone in my home as I write this. I have a difficult time containing my emotions!

Everyone has said this was the correct decision to have Florence cared for at Serenity Heights, and no one could have a better place to live than she does. Ilene and Bob have been so impressed that their family made the decision to move their mom, Katie, to Serenity as well. She is now Florence's roommate.

The Serenity Heights home is the best I've ever seen

I have been in the ministry for sixty-nine years and in and out of many wonderful care facilities, but never have I found all of the desired and valued qualities in one home such as in Serenity Heights.

I have quality time with Florence each day before lunch. We read the paper together, make phone calls, and take care of personal things together just as we would have done at home. Every evening we go through our mail, and at our age and with our many involvements, we have a lot of mail! This takes us an hour or so, except on the nights when our Clippers basketball team is playing; then that is the priority!

Florence and I attend church and Bible class each Sunday I am in town. Our bus system has very inexpensive bus service, so it is a good, safe way of transporting Florence in her wheelchair.

I am still expecting that Florence will improve to the extent that she will come back home to live; however, in the meantime, even amid tears and loneliness, Romans 8:28 becomes a wonderful comfort and guide: "We know that God works for good in everything with those who love Him, who are called according to His purpose."

70 Years of Family

Ninety-Fifth Birthday Celebration

CONCLUSION

THE MOST EXCEPTIONAL AND PHENOMENAL EVENT

As I look back over my shoulder, no other event, past or in the future, could ever change the world as much as Easter did.

Easter proves it!
First: There are no final good-byes between Christians.
Second: We shall live after death.
Third: The God power that raised Christ from the grave will raise us. This is promised to us in 1 Corinthians 6:14.

Isn't it great to be in our wonderful America, which our godly fore-fathers established on God's Word and His commandments? I adore the flags of nations influenced by Christianity. Many show all three colors, red, white, and blue. On our American flag especially, *white* was the color for God the Father and of purity as it related to the reality of God. The color *red* signified the Messiah's shedding of blood and the atonement through the promised Messiah. *Blue* was the color of the Holy Spirit because He was the revealer of the truth.

Above every thought, plan, dream, and far beyond any happiness on earth or heaven is the resurrection of God's only Son, Jesus, who was both man and God on earth!

The entire Christian church throughout the world, numbering about one-third of the population, agree that it is the most far-reaching and powerful thing that could ever happen to influence every man and woman who has ever lived on earth!

Of all books ever written, with its drama and lifesaving passages, the Bible tops them all!

Easter proves God's entire plan revealed in the Bible!
I have visited the Holy Land seven times, and each time we have gone to the empty tomb where they placed the body of our Lord and Savior Jesus Christ, who did not stay on the cross or in this grave—*He arose! Praise God!*

God Promises through Easter that Jesus Christ is the Son of God.
Romans 1:4: "And who through the Spirit of holiness was appointed the Son of God in power by His resurrection from the dead: Jesus Christ our Lord."

God promises that we shall live after death and be happy forever.
1 Corinthians 6:14: "By His power, God raised the Lord from the dead and He will raise us also."

God proves through Easter that everyone faces judgment.
However, for the Christian, we have no fears; we have the hope of heaven.

John 11:25: "He that believeth in Me though he were dead, yet shall he live. Whoever lives and believes in me shall never die."

What a wonderful, glorious day it will be!

About The Author

Dr. Orville G. Hiepler was born on a farm near Springbrook, North Dakota, in 1920 to Gustav and Anna Hiepler. He attended a one-room schoolhouse and high school in Epping, North Dakota. His undergraduate work was at Concordia College in Moorhead, Minnesota, and his postgraduate work was at Luther Seminary in St. Paul, Minnesota. Studies at Union Biblical Seminary in New York City, UCLA, and the Graduate School of Theology all contributed to his PhD. Summer courses at Lutheran Bible School in Seattle, evangelism training in Florida, and serving as the evangelist at Preaching, Teaching, Reaching missions contributed to his Bible knowledge and his knowledge of mission work. He was on the Los Angeles Mayor's Senior Citizen Committee; was on the Lutheran Social Services Board of North and Southern California; was the chairperson of the Ministerial Association in Camarillo, California; was a Rotary International member; and was president of the Fallbrook Golf Club and various committees and boards. He has served churches in Pasco, Washington; Sacramento, California; Hawthorne, California; Camarillo, California; and Oceanside, California and has assisted in churches in Wisconsin, North Dakota, and Tennessee. Dr. Hiepler planted and grew churches and schools and has served as a school principal as well during his tenure. Dr. Hiepler has been married to his wife, Florence, for seventy years. He has four children, ten grandchildren, and eight great-grandchildren. He and Florence have led sixteen tours to various places around the world. He is the author of *The Pastor-Administrator: The Key to Growth and Vitality*. Dr. Hiepler and Florence reside in Camarillo, California.

Orville with his puppy Rover

Unbelievable things have happened in one life time. Things have changed very little from the time of Christ up until a hundred years ago. From the invention of cars and planes, to computers and the digital age, Orville has been here to watch most of this transformation. He's written down some of his experiences in this book, we hope you enjoy the journey of reliving some of the highlights!

Orville with is horse Blackie, the fastest horse around!

Dr. Reverend Orville Hiepler is a Lutheran pastor who has served in congregations from his home state of North Dakota to Washington and California. He is a father of four children, husband to Florence, and brother to five wonderful sisters. Orville is the most energetic man you will ever meet. He's always inviting strangers to the dinner table, chatting to people in line and encouraging people where ever he goes. He is truly a man after Gods own heart and is passionate about sharing with anyone how living a life with Christ is the most fun adventure, a quite extraordinary one!

-Kari Bradberry (Granddaughter)

Cover photo: from Florence's Parental farm home. Father, relatives and little brother at the crank.
Jacket design: *by Kari Bradberry*
Inside Jacket couple portrait: *Bob Loranger*